MW00988061

"After spending more than seve both marketplace and ministry temptations offered by ego anc and brilliant thought leader Nicole Massie Martin offers a new paradigm that is centered on the sacrificial example of Jesus. I am grateful for this book, and you will be too!"
Nona Jones, preacher, business leader, and author of *The Gift of Rejection*

"The most helpful, practical, challenging, inspiring, and empowering leadership book I've read. In *Nailing It*, Nicole Massie Martin has provided a blueprint for effective leadership in our rapidly changing world. By identifying leadership practices that hinder our effectiveness and sharing practical principles that lead to personal and organizational flourishing, Nicole has 'nailed' the pressing leadership issues of our day."
Christine Caine, founder of A21 and Propel Women

"Nicole Massie Martin offers a unique approach to leadership, one that recognizes the pathways and pitfalls of current leadership models in the church and in the culture, but one that also challenges various approaches with the perspective of a leader crucified to self for the glory of God and the good of those they lead. Every leader will resonate with one or more of the issues raised, and every leader will be helped by the wisdom offered in these pages."
Ed Stetzer, dean at the Talbot School of Theology, Biola University

"Nicole Massie Martin's *Nailing It* shines a light on the approaches that are needed now and in the future. I loved Nicole's focus on inclusion in leadership with clear examples of women and people of color. Through founding 4word, I have witnessed how leaders in companies like Toyota North America (through its Christian Fellowship), Envision Radiology, Escalante Golf, and many others implement transformational characteristics of love, surrender, grace, and trust. *Nailing It* offers practical approaches for leaders to implement these qualities. In addition, *Nailing It* provides hope for the future where the love of Christ can be shared by leaders of tomorrow by their example with those who may never enter the doors of a church or know another follower of Christ."
Diane Paddison, founder of 4word and former global executive with Fortune 500 and Fortune 1000 companies

"*Nailing It* is a clarion call for leaders to resist the pull toward ego, power hoarding, and toxic leadership and receive the invitation to follow in Jesus' footsteps and become servant leaders who are meek and lead with low egos to make a great impact."
Ekemini Uwan, public theologian

"By reading this book, you can learn from one of the most impressive and effective leaders in the world today. Regardless of your specific calling, Nicole Massie Martin here will equip you to lead with joy, humility, and excellence while overcoming discouragement and hardship. By the time you close the book, you will not only be ready to lead better, but you will also be inspired to follow Jesus more closely than ever."

Russell Moore, editor in chief at Christianity Today and author of *Losing Our Religion: An Altar Call for Evangelical America*

"*Nailing It* is a powerful and timely look at an approach to leadership that challenges the status quo and invites leaders into a deeper, more authentic way of leading. Nicole Massie Martin nails it when she boldly states that true leadership must flow from crucified lives, allowing God's healing and grace to be resurrected in and through us. She masterfully critiques the inadequacies of our current leadership models and offers a compelling vision for where we could and should aspire to be."

John K. Jenkins Sr., senior pastor at First Baptist Church of Glenarden in Landover, Maryland

"An encounter with my dear sister Nicole Massie Martin is always an uplifting experience. This book is no exception. While sobering, it challenges the secular reaches of leadership with the call for crucified leadership. Martin presents a well-organized, logical progression of leadership issues with thoughtful principles and some personal reflections. May all of us who have the privilege of leadership follow the path outlined in this book where we crucify those bad habits and patterns and resurrect God's glorious intentions as we serve him and his people!"

Bob Doll, CEO of Crossmark Global Investments

"If you've asked yourself how you can respond to the triple challenges of suffering, trauma, and anxiety, this is the book for you. In *Nailing It*, we are invited to reimagine our Christian leadership to a cruciformity that can heal and transform a generation. The cross still points the way!"

Gabriel Salguero, president of the National Latino Evangelical Coalition

"In *Nailing It*, Nicole Massey Martin brings us to the heart of leadership rooted in the cross. With wisdom, authenticity, and grace, she shows that true leadership flows from sacrifice, humility, and surrender to Jesus. This is a must-read for anyone longing to lead like Christ in a self-centered world."

Derwin L. Gray, cofounder and lead pastor of Transformation Church and author of *Lit Up with Love*

NAILING IT

WHY SUCCESSFUL LEADERSHIP
DEMANDS
SUFFERING AND SURRENDER

NICOLE MASSIE MARTIN

FOREWORD BY CAREY NIEUWHOF

An imprint of InterVarsity Press
Downers Grove, Illinois

InterVarsity Press
P.O. Box 1400 | Downers Grove, IL 60515-1426
ivpress.com | email@ivpress.com

©2025 by Nicole Massie Martin

All rights reserved. No part of this book may be reproduced in any form without written permission from InterVarsity Press.

InterVarsity Press® is the publishing division of InterVarsity Christian Fellowship/USA®. For more information, visit intervarsity.org.

All Scripture quotations, unless otherwise indicated, are taken from The Holy Bible, New International Version®, NIV®. Copyright © 1973, 1978, 1984, 2011 by Biblica, Inc.™ Used by permission of Zondervan. All rights reserved worldwide. www.zondervan.com. The "NIV" and "New International Version" are trademarks registered in the United States Patent and Trademark Office by Biblica, Inc.™

While any stories in this book are true, some names and identifying information may have been changed to protect the privacy of individuals.

Author photo by Imiivo Photo Studios

Interior image: ©Big Ryan / DigitalVision Vectors

The publisher cannot verify the accuracy or functionality of website URLs used in this book beyond the date of publication.

Cover design: Faceout Studio, Addie Lutzo
Interior design: Jeanna Wiggins

ISBN 978-1-5140-0974-1 (print) | ISBN 978-1-5140-0975-8 (digital)

Printed in the United States of America ∞

Library of Congress Cataloging-in-Publication Data
Names: Martin, Nicole (Nicole Massie), author.
Title: Nailing it : why successful leadership demands suffering and
    surrender / Nicole Massie Martin.
Description: Downers Grove, IL : IVP, [2025] | Includes bibliographical
    references.
Identifiers: LCCN 2024043501 (print) | LCCN 2024043502 (ebook) | ISBN
    9781514009741 (print) | ISBN 9781514009758 (digital)
Subjects: LCSH: Christian leadership.
Classification: LCC BV652.1 .M234 2025 (print) | LCC BV652.1 (ebook) |
    DDC 253–dc23/eng/20241115
LC record available at https://lccn.loc.gov/2024043501
LC ebook record available at https://lccn.loc.gov/2024043502

31 30 29 28 27 26 25 | 12 11 10 9 8 7 6 5 4 3 2 1

To young leaders looking for new ways of being,

to seasoned leaders looking for new inspiration,

to believers yearning for new models for living,

to those searching for God—

this book is dedicated to you.

In honor of my amazing father,

Rev. Leonard P. Massie Jr.

(1950–2022)

CONTENTS

FOREWORD

Carey Nieuwhof

"Leadership is designed to kill you."

The statement jumped off the page at me.

At first glance, it explains so much. We live in a time when an alarming number of pastors, church leaders, and prominent Christian figures rarely reach the end of their tenure without experiencing some form of crisis or breakdown. Leadership, it seems, *is* killing us.

Or consider the growing trend of church leaders who don't just encounter crises—they resign, often quietly, in despair or frustration. Others are forced out by moral failures that seem to happen with frightening regularity. Every time I think we've seen the last scandal in the church, another one emerges, and then another. Sometimes I hear of three in a day. Ugh.

But it's not just moral failure that's taking leaders down.

The overwhelming demands of leadership are crushing families and draining the life out of leaders. Over time, these leaders become shadows of the people they once were or, worse, they simply quit. Their calling wasn't finished, but they were.

To say that Christian leadership is in crisis is not an overstatement.

This brings us back to the idea that leadership is designed to kill us. But what does that really mean? Is leadership some sort of conspiracy, meant to claim more victims than victors? Is it inevitable that if you sign up to serve God in your calling, you'll end up as another statistic?

There's another way to understand this premise, and it's where the promise of this book lies.

Leadership—Christian leadership, specifically—is not designed to kill all of you but rather the parts of you that need to die.

After all, Jesus said to his closest followers, "Among you it will be different" (Matthew 20:26 NLT).

So why isn't Christian leadership different? That's the great question that Nicole Martin so helpfully (and painfully) explores.

If you do it right, Christian leadership should kill your thirst for power, your ego, the relentless pace driven by your ambition, your insatiable desire to perform, your quest for perfection, the unreasonable demands you place on others to be loyal to you, and your secret desire to see your ministry scale and gain prominence.

When these ambitions die, something far more powerful rises.

This is the critical difference between Christian leadership and leadership driven by secular values. Unfortunately, the latter have seeped into Christian leadership like arsenic. It doesn't take a lot of toxins to kill you. Even a small dose of noncrucified metrics—success, scale, and performance motivated by ego—can be deadly.

I've felt this battle in my own leadership journey. Early on I rarely questioned my motives. After all, I had left a promising career in law to enter ministry. That was an altruistic move, right? So how could my motives be anything *but* pure?

But the longer I've led and the deeper I've gone in following Jesus, the more I've realized my motives are far from pure. Sadly, they're often mixed, sometimes deeply so. I've been obsessed with performance, both mine and others. I've loved the idea of scaling ministry. For years I operated at a speed that no human could sustain. That lasted until my body declared a finish line because I didn't—I burned out.

When I read the stories of leaders who have fallen, I recognize that the seeds of failure exist within me too. A little less self-discipline, a bit more distance from community, or a few steps away from Christ, and I grow frightened to think what I might be capable of.

Leadership is designed to kill you if you do it right, by nailing all your passions and ambitions to the cross.

That's what (I hope) I'm in the process of doing, nailing all of that.

As you read through this perceptive book, I pray that you, as I did, see the parts of yourself that still need to die.

And don't get discouraged; there will *always* be parts.

Sanctification is a lifelong journey. The Christian leadership journey is, to use a phrase coined by Friedrich Nietzsche and popularized by Eugene Peterson, a long obedience in the same direction.

However, as you die to the things that both cause death and deserve death, you will find the very thing Jesus promised—life, and life in all its fullness. The church needs that now more than ever, as does the world.

Introduction

THE TIME IS NOW

This book may not make you money. It's unlikely to increase your status, get you the next best job, or bring you into new stratospheres of power. This is the book you pick up when you finally realize that traditional leadership no longer works for who you are or for the people you serve. For generations, leaders have been encouraged to wear leadership like a store-bought suit and to simply tailor it to fit our contexts. We've believed the idea that good leadership is about getting things done and that teams are designed to help us get there.

And then came millennials who started demanding more from their workplaces. No longer satisfied with simply doing a job, they pushed their organizations to actually care. They grew weary of narratives where leaders and staff members went to places they hated just for a paycheck and strived to belong to places that valued who they were beyond what they did.

And then came greater diversity. Traditional leadership teachings and styles hung on predominantly White male models that were assumed to fit every lifestyle. But women needed room for their natural gifts to shine, and people of color needed space to elevate the values they brought into their roles. Even White men grew weary of the leadership status quo, craving innovative ways to lean into changing realities. This increased the need for new, more comprehensive models of leadership to accommodate this newer, more diverse leadership landscape.

And then came the Covid-19 pandemic. Prior to March 2020, it was almost unheard of to consider how an employee felt or what they needed in order to work effectively. But when entire workforces were required to work from home and people had space to think more carefully about what it meant to do a job, things began to change. Motivations for work changed. How people felt about teams changed. The willingness to acknowledge mental health and to create environments for flourishing changed, and this was not limited to just one industry. Every organization was affected by this gradual shift from a mission-centric to a people-centric workplace. None of these factors are negative in and of themselves, but each brings new challenges and opportunities to rethink the way we've always done leadership.

These and many other shifts have affected every area of business, even reaching to churches and faith-based organizations where work fatigue increased with changes in society. Volunteers have started to expect more from the places where they serve. Faith-based staff members are carrying greater responsibilities and experiencing higher levels of burnout. When you add increased visibility through social media and the gut-wrenching stories of moral failures among leaders, what you get is a leadership crisis. There are greater demands on leaders to serve with compassion than in the past and greater awareness of the impact of toxicity in the workplace. In both secular and sacred spaces, there is a deficit of leaders who operate with integrity in their empathy and a proliferation of wounded employees. How can we bridge the gap between the lack of strong leadership and the overabundance of needs? The only way to solve this is to shift the way Christian leaders think about leadership in order to shift the way they lead.

The emphasis of this book is on Christian leaders for several reasons:

1. *Christian leaders are located everywhere.* They serve in the church, at the bank, in schools, and in just about every field imaginable. Christian leaders have the greatest capacity to reach the largest amount of people in the world.

2. *Christian leaders ought to be guided by principles that go beyond their occupations.* Regardless of where they serve, Christian leaders theoretically answer to a higher calling. This allows them to be centrally influenced by the gospel in a way that makes them more open to God-directed changes and pivots.

3. *Christianity itself is in crisis.* While Christian leaders are everywhere, what we observe across the ecclesiastical landscape is a type of identity crisis within churches where even the people inside of them have no idea who they are. We have lost sight of what it means to be lights in darkness. We have forgotten what it means to prioritize the needs of the least of these, elevating internal needs over those in the church's community. As a result, we have lost sight of what it means to be a disciple and follower of Jesus. This crisis creates a vacuum where it is easier to learn a new trade than it is to learn how to follow Christ.

4. *We have disconnected faith from discomfort and leadership from sacrifice.* At the core of Christianity is the cross, and at the core of leadership is servitude. When both are in crisis, the default is to lean toward what is comfortable and easy. But it is a dangerous world when leaders care more about their comfort than their calling and when faith is more about height than it is about depth.

5. *God is the only one who can solve the crises we face in society and in our lives.* Self-help books will not solve the deeper issues. Doing what we've always done will simply get us the same results. Only God can prompt us to redirect our lives in a way that brings healing and hope to the world. Without him, we can do nothing.

Now more than ever, we need courageous Christian leaders in every field who are willing to turn to God for a revelatory vision of how to lead in times of intense trauma. We need people who don't mind taking up their crosses to follow Christ, not only to the mountain tops but also into the valleys of pain. We need a revival of crucified living that might take us to resurrected leadership for the glory of God and the good of the people! But necessary tasks hardly ever come easy.

A PREVIEW OF THE JOURNEY

We are about to begin an excursion together to wrestle with what it looks like to lead with crucified lives so that a truer vision of God's healing grace may be resurrected in and through us. I am defining the "crucified life" as the day by day, moment by moment process of taking up our crosses to follow Jesus. Some scholars, such as Michael Gorman, have used the term *cruciformity* to describe this process of "letting the cross of the crucified Messiah be the shape, as well as the source, of life in him."[1] Since *crucifixion* names the finished work of Christ on the cross and *cruciformity* names the spiritual discipline of being shaped by the cross, it's important to use both terms to illuminate the true glory of resurrection. This journey will invite you to rethink your context, your capacity, and your calling in ways that are designed to make you unsettled enough for God to do something new. As much as it would be easier for God to do miraculous works in our lives when things are smooth, disruption is the primary means to bring about lasting change. If you're ready, we will walk together to disrupt our previous ideas about leadership, crucifying them on the cross, and making room for God to resurrect visions of healing in their place. Here's how we'll do it.

In the first section, we'll unpack the problem of why the world feels more stressed and traumatized now than ever before. We'll explore some of the themes mentioned above that have contributed to our current crises and get real about dangers of American triumphalism. While the context is carefully structured for Americans, there is no doubt that principles of power, ego, performance, and more can be applied across global contexts. The purpose of discussing the roots of the issues is to build the courage to figure out what we can do about it.

In the second section, we'll take time to investigate the progression from where we are to where we want to be. We'll wade through seven areas of traditional leadership that will need to be reframed through the lens of crucifixion and resurrection. I will regularly use the phrase *traditional leadership,* knowing that each element presents itself in various forms of leadership teaching and philosophies. We'll begin with larger concepts, including power and ego. These will set the stage for looking at our motivations to lead. From there, we'll move to more internal challenges of reconsidering speed, performance, and perfection. After this, we'll shift to organizational perspectives on loyalty and scale. Throughout each of these chapters, you'll see a combination of stories from fictional accounts to historic reflections to futuristic projections to define what's at stake. While we may experience some natural turbulence that comes from tussling with the past, we'll land the plane with either questions to reflect on or summary points you may consider.

The last section is all about the promise of God for those who are willing to take the leap of faith into new leadership realities. You'll see Jesus as the center point for most of the scriptural application, but this last chapter will expand to deepen our biblical basis of hope. We'll dream together to find out what is possible and be encouraged to know that we are not alone. In the end, my hope is that you will finish this book with greater conviction to lay it all down before Christ who can raise up something more glorious through you.

MY PRAYER FOR YOU

I cannot tell you how honored I am to guide you on this journey! As I've written these words, I've had each of you in mind: those who are already leading and looking for new paths, those who are considering leadership and aren't certain of where to start, and those who have taken on nontraditional forms of leadership in volunteer organizations, in your churches, and even in your homes. I've been praying for you. With each paragraph and with each story, I've asked God to speak uniquely to you in ways that might help you to hear him. I know that my words are feeble, and I'm certain that there are things I've overlooked. But my earnest prayer is that there might be something in these pages that challenges the way you've thought or acted and prompts you toward a new vision for yourself and for those you serve.

I've had the privilege of serving in a variety of leadership roles: in student government, in the school orchestra, on the junior usher board, in the choir, and on the playground during school. I've led young adults, Sunday school teachers, life group leaders, preachers, and staff members as an executive minister. I've led churches in city mobilization and regions as a national director. I've led large groups as a senior vice president and small groups as the discipleship pastor. I've started organizations as the executive director and helped build others as a trustee, executive committee teammate, and board member. I've served in the C-suite as a chief impact officer and found my most challenging and fulfilling roles as a wife, mother, sister, daughter, granddaughter, niece, cousin, and friend. But none of these roles would be possible without the prayers of the saints and the merciful power of God. If you are willing and ready, I believe that your hardest days of leadership might prove to be the most redemptive times of faith in Christ. I cannot wait to see what God has in store. Let's have some fun!

PART 1

THE

PROBLEM

1

THE REALITIES OF STRESS AND SUFFERING IN OUR PRESENT AGE

COMPOUNDED PERSONAL STRESS

It was Friday at 6:13 p.m. He kept telling himself that he would stop after that one last email, but there were so many "lasts" that he lost count. He needed to respond to the issue that came up about the building so that everyone could get into the office on Monday. He had to reply to the legal team to make sure the organization was properly protected. He had no choice but to reply to one of his direct reports about a personnel issue that would likely lead to a dispute. He knew he could not ignore the message from the finance team asking for salaries and headcounts to determine the next steps in a potential reduction in force.

Like a good teacher, he answered each email in turn, responding as directly as possible, resolving each question quickly so that the next problem could step forward. This was how he was taught by his predecessor. "Real leaders start early and stay late" was the refrain that echoed in his head every time his eyes fought against the heaviness of exhaustion. His brain was beginning to enter the fog zone as answers jumbled together and words lost their distinction. He had just been promoted to the C-suite above his peers, and it felt like they were all waiting to see him fail. But it was difficult to juggle the demands of a new job with the increasing demands of his aging mother. He moved into her neighborhood a few months ago to make sure he could check on her frequently, but her memory loss seemed to be more prevalent with each passing week. When he brought her dinner after yet another late night at work, he was heartbroken to hear her call him by the neighbor's name. With so much stress in the office and so much stress at home, his life felt like an unstable stack of Jenga blocks, just waiting to fall on the next turn.

It was Thursday at 2:55 p.m. She sat at her computer with her to-do list on the left, food behind the screen, and two stale cups of coffee on the right. She had fifty-five tabs open on her screen, all demanding immediate attention. Her work screen reflected emails that needed responses, messages from colleagues that were still unread, and a task list that reprimanded her every time she saw it, rebuking her for all the boxes left unchecked while new tasks waited impatiently to be added. Her "side-hustle" screen revealed the fact that she was far too busy to even have a side hustle, but the necessary items left in her Amazon shopping cart said otherwise. Her "kids' stuff" screen was also open, punishing her for not staying on top of school supplies or camp registrations that would soon accumulate late fees. Her Zoom screen was in full-blown meeting mode, but she had perfected the art of keeping her eyes in one place, hoping that her colleagues could not tell that she was also responding to a text from her sister at the same time.

When her phone rang, she noticed the time and realized how quickly 8 a.m. turned to 2:55 p.m., which was five minutes past the time to leave the house and pick up the kids. With thoughts scattered, heart racing, and so much left undone, she typed her goodbye in the Zoom chat and grabbed her keys, knowing that all the screens she'd left behind would be anxiously awaiting her return.

I wonder if anything in these stories resonates with you. Maybe you can identify with what it means to juggle the demands of work and family at the same time. Perhaps you understand what it feels like to carry the invisible burdens of weighty decisions that keep you up at night. No one has to tell you that we are living in stressful times because you already know it. You feel it every time you wake up and fight it every time you lie down.

Stress can be defined differently for each of us and can be triggered in a variety of ways. My stress often comes from my inability to say no and from my tendency to take on more than I can possibly do at one time. Your stress may come from relationships or work or other areas that trigger the worst parts of who you are. Regardless of its origin or nature, every single one of us experiences stress of some kind during various parts of our days. For the most part, stress can be a helpful motivator to drive us to get things done and to move things along in our lives. Yet, for many of us, stress can be a distraction from ourselves, from others, and even from God. When we are stressed, we cannot focus on other people and often struggle to figure out our needs. At the peak of our stress, when we are most in need of God, we are also most prone to turn away from God, trying to find quick fixes to problems that only God can solve. While humanity has always struggled with the daily challenges of work, care for family, personal health, and communal well-being, you and I must now deal with the compounded nature of these stressors. The simplicity of dealing with one stress at a time is gone and the complexity of simultaneously navigating multiple realities has come.

Take the 2020 pandemic, for example. It was never simply that the Covid-19 virus spread and extended quarantines were distressing. It was also the fact that the pandemic piled on top of family stress, which sat on top of pre-existing emotional trauma, which sat on top of relationship strains and difficulties at work and lack of connection at church and everything else. Nations have always had socioeconomic disparities, but the lack of natural resources today and lack of access for those most impoverished seems to have grown over time. Communities have always wrestled with divisions, but the overexposure to media coupled with the algorithms that keep people talking to people like themselves have expanded the walls that divide us today. While humanity has always wrestled with a multiplicity of tensions, what we feel and experience now is what some might call "a perfect stress storm" with potential to affect us internally and externally, personally and collectively, nationally and globally. And this is what we bring with us to the workplace.

Chances are that you already know this. You can tell that people on your teams are a little more on edge now than they were before. Meetings seem a little more strained now than they were before 2019. Colleagues may seem more sensitive, more easily offended, more likely to be absent physically, emotionally, or mentally. This was especially true in 2021 when management professor Anthony Klotz coined the phrase "the Great Resignation."[1] At that time, he anticipated that the increase of four unique trends at the height of the pandemic would lead to a massive resignation of the American workforce. He attributed this phenomenon to "an existing backlog of resignations as some workers chose to stay in their jobs because of the uncertainty resulting from the pandemic, widespread burnout among workers, widespread re-evaluation of priorities and values among workers and the reluctance of some workers to give up remote work."[2] While Klotz believed the resignations would eventually subside as workplaces became more tolerable and people found themselves in more meaningful roles, the lingering effects of this moment in history will take many years to resolve. In the past, we could get away with not focusing as much on the needs of the workforce, believing that a paycheck would be enough to keep employees engaged. Instead, this new reality teaches us that people are demanding more from their workplaces and even more from faith-based organizations where they serve. And when they do not receive what they need, they will resign or, even worse, quit quietly.

This idea of "quiet quitting" followed the trends of the Great Resignation with employees checking out of jobs they did not want. In 2022, Gallup found that more than 50 percent of the American workforce had quietly quit, performing at bare minimum levels for their jobs or less.[3] They were unwilling to do anything more than what was listed on the job description, silently separating themselves from any organizational affiliation. This was a significant problem because it signaled a noteworthy disconnect between employees and employers.[4] People became less engaged with their organizations because they did not feel that their work mattered. They did not feel cared for, they did not have clear expectations, they did not have pathways for growth, and they no longer felt part of something meaningful.

This was especially true for younger workers who were often at lower positions within organizations. During the pandemic, they felt even more isolated from their workplaces and colleagues, creating a greater rift between them and the people around them. They became disillusioned, lacking the mentorship and guidance necessary for future success. This only compounded the stress affecting younger workers and increased their anxieties around life and work. According to the American College Health Association, college graduates are entering the workplace with higher levels of anxiety and depression than the generations that preceded them.[5] They have learned to survive work, but their acute awareness of mental health makes them unlikely to thrive or to stay when the workplace becomes emotionally unhealthy.

Women also experienced increased stress during the pandemic and in the years that followed. Women with children found themselves doing everything imaginable during the pandemic when many children were in virtual school at home. They were acting as coach, counselor, teacher, housekeeper, chef, and more, all while trying to maintain some sense of sanity themselves. Single women often kept longer work hours during the pandemic with less time or space to connect with friends or participate in community. Loneliness among women skyrocketed as social spaces became more limited, and many women began turning to other comforts to ease the pain. In 2019, the National Institute of Health found that rates of alcohol use disorder (AUD) increased in women by 84 percent over the past ten years relative to a 35 percent increase in men.[6] The normalization of alcohol use as a means of coping with stress was already rising before 2020, making this pandemic the perfect storm for the rise in alcohol-related deaths among women.[7] While some of these realities will subside over time, the lingering effects of these challenges will continue for many years to come, reshaping the workplace as we have known it.

The pandemic also proved to be stressful for some ethnic and racial groups, specifically in Black, Asian, Jewish, and Latino communities. In early 2020, news that the spread of Covid-19 originated in China led to a rise in hate crimes against Asian Americans.[8] People wanted someone to blame and felt like Asians were ideal targets for their pain. While Black Americans remain the most targeted group for hate crimes, they too saw an increase in traumatic murders and hate crimes during this season. Millions of people watched as George Floyd's life was snuffed out as he suffocated under a police officer's knee, further underscoring the racialization of death for petty crimes. Black men dying for small infractions has become a common occurrence in America, and while some called 2020 a year of "racial reckoning," others felt that nothing changed. Jewish communities also faced increasing fear of crimes against them as antisemitic rhetoric and crimes rose as much as 36 percent in the years following the pandemic.[9] The growing harassment online seemed to be bolstered by political agendas that made even synagogues feel unsafe. Anti-immigration sentiments also grew, affecting Latino communities across the United States. Even those who grew up in America felt the tensions of victimization. These growing crimes and mounting statistics have created an environment of fear and lack of trust that affects how many people show up for work each day.

As if that weren't enough, Americans are experiencing the collective stress of growing political divides. In 2020, Pew Research found that more than two-thirds of the country believed we were more divided than we were before the pandemic. We are divided not only by who we vote for but also by the demonization of the other side. In 2020, 89 percent of Donald Trump supporters felt that Joe Biden's election would lead to lasting harm to our country, while

90 percent of Biden supporters felt the exact same about Trump.[10] The deep divisions of politics made everything feel political, from vaccines to criminal justice and even decisions made about schools. These strains were so palpable in families and in churches that people found themselves unable to have conversations with others who did not see things as they did. The idea of civil dialogue was nearly lost as violence grew against those with opposing views. This was no longer an issue of differing opinions. This felt like a division of values and expectations, affecting how we live, how we lead, and yes, even how we work together.

The stressors of our times are so expansive that it would be impossible to name them all. We can go through every category of people, every major life event, and every organizational flaw to find what we already know: stress affects us all in different ways and at different times. What is unique about this time is the fact that organizations and workplaces are not immune to the impacts of individual stress and trauma. In the past, leadership remained somewhat inoculated from the challenges of life around it, believing that leaders who were consistent in the pursuit of vision would most certainly succeed. But the stress and challenges of our times have caused a fundamental shift in how we show up in the world, how we show up in the workplace, and therefore, how we lead in the midst of it. We can no longer lead teams as if everyone is the same. We can no longer lead blindly, as if race, gender, age, politics, or other differences do not matter. Doing so would run the risk of compounding the stress people are already experiencing, making the workplace potentially more toxic and the organization's mission less likely to be achieved. Instead, the best way to lead in times of immense stress, trauma, and pressure is not to avoid it but to enter into it. Rather than to ignore the stress that affects us and others, perhaps the calling from God is to enter into that stress as means of bringing radical redemption and hope for times like these.

A THEOLOGY OF ENTERING IN

The scariest part about a haunted house is going inside. When you're standing outside, you can see what you are about to enter. The decor is so disinviting that everything around the house literally screams, "Do not enter!" Those who are crazy enough to take steps forward often do so at their own risk. They may even see a sign or hear a voice that says, "Enter if you dare," but if you can make it through the door, you're more than halfway through.

Knowing that Jesus entered humanity through his birth almost feels like entering a haunted house. I imagine the darkness of the world and the sin of humanity felt a lot like the signs and sounds that screamed, "Enter if you dare!" The risk of entrusting divinity in humanity was extremely high as light became life and Spirit took on flesh. But, despite the warning signs and the dangers, Jesus dared to enter the world haunted by sin to prove his love for all creation. He entered into the stress of the times, choosing to be born to a family that didn't even have enough money for a proper room. While he could have magically appeared as a conquering adult king, he chose to enter this world through the stress and strain of childbirth, appearing as a helpless child. He entered into the tensions of both birthrights and adoptive care, coming directly from God by way of the Holy Spirit, through Mary and cared for by Joseph. The stress of his birth was compounded by the stress of the required census, which was compounded by the vulnerable position of the Jews under the Romans, which was compounded by the complexities of a covenantal promise and the Jews' faith in a coming Messiah.

The incarnation of Christ is God's voluntary acknowledgment of humanity's stress. Being born in a stressful time, in a stressful manner, was one of the many ways that God demonstrated his understanding of the traumas that negatively affect our lives. He did not choose to stand apart from our stress, though that would have certainly been an easier route. Instead, he chose to stand with us in our stress, being born as we are born, struggling as we struggle, taking in both personal and communal realities that cause stress to every generation. And yet, because he was born into this stress, his birth became the pathway to our redemption. Through his birth, Jesus modeled that even the most stressful situations can be redeemed and our darkest nights of pain can turn into the brightest days of hope.

In the first words of his Gospel account, John illustrated the redemption that happened when Jesus entered in. Mirroring the language of Genesis, John described Jesus as the Word who was in the beginning with God and who was God (John 1:1-2). He went on to say that Jesus was not only the

Word, he was also the incarnation of life, which is the light to shine in the darkness of our humanity (John 1:4-5). This light, John says, will shine in the darkness but will not be overcome by it. It will be present in pain but not overwhelmed by it. The light of Christ will exist in times of intense stress and struggle but will not be overtaken by them. By taking on flesh and dwelling among us, Jesus as the Word, the life, and the light modeled his power both to understand and transform everything we experience in this world (John 1:14). He simultaneously validated and diminished the darkness by showing up as light. As the One who is life and gives eternal life, Jesus validated and defeated death as we know it. With just his miraculous presence through incarnation, Jesus became the One who both understood us and changed us for all eternity.

Incarnation teaches us the value of validating our realities to diminish their power in the presence of God. But the only way to fully experience the redemptive power of this life as light is to fully understand the depths of the darkness. We have an invitation from God to understand stress and suffering by entering it as a means of redeeming it. While we cannot always change the things that stress us, we can expose them to the truth of God's Word so that he can redeem them for our good. Every stress and every struggle can be redeemed for God's glory and our good! Therefore, when we enter the realities of stress around us and take time to understand what people are going through, we make room for God to redeem that stress for God's glory and our good. We enter into the pain of suffering when we learn the challenges that others face and are willing to understand with empathy and grace. Renowned psychologist and trauma counselor Diane Langberg said, "We are called to enter into relationships centered on suffering so that we might reveal in flesh and blood the nature of the Crucified One."[11] When we enter the pain and suffering of others, we also enter the pain and suffering of Christ who stands in solidarity with us. This presence in suffering is not just for the sake of unity and comradery but for the purpose of redemption, bringing creativity, healing, and hope.

Every relationship presents us with an opportunity to enter the realities of others as Christ entered our realities through his birth. As leaders, we enter not simply to validate and understand but also to transform and create together what no one could create alone. Leadership that is both empathic and redemptive makes room to see people where they are while simultaneously bringing them to where they could be. This powerful experience allows team members, volunteers, and staff to feel seen and heard, giving them greater motivation to serve and grow with others. But the opposite is also true when leaders refuse to enter the stress and suffering of others. By rejecting the opportunity to enter in, we run the risk of assuming that everyone is just like us. We short-circuit our compassion by not truly understanding who and where people are. We limit our connections with shallow conversations that hardly ever allow people to be seen or heard. In the workplace, leaders who refuse to enter the stress of others are more likely to run them over, using them like tools in a toolbox that can be easily replaced when they wear down. This further exacerbates stress for those who are most vulnerable, making them less effective for themselves, for their team, and even for God.

Entering the pain, stress, and trauma of others requires that we see our teams and organizations as places of healing and not simply places of work. It might sound idealistic, but given the depth of trauma that faces each generation and the intensity of stress that mounts with every passing moment, this might be a significant factor for employee recruitment and retention for years to come. People want to work where they feel valued and seen. They want to serve in contexts where leaders care about who they are and not just about what they do. Workplaces with demonstrative empathy and compassion are far more successful at keeping and recruiting new team members than those who are not. In this way, entering into the stress and pain of others is not simply good theology, it's also good sense.

DEBUNKING EMPATHY MYTHS

If entering into the stress and realties of others helps increase employee engagement, then why doesn't it happen more often, especially in Christian workplaces? Unfortunately, while the motivators for doing what is right may be clear, the incentive for doing what is wrong is often very appealing. The only way to change organizational and leadership behaviors is by naming the myths and lies we tend to believe and beginning the process of replacing them with the truth. As we consider the importance of entering in, here are a few common misplaced reasons why we don't, and what we can do about them:

1. *Entering the stress and realities of others validates their dysfunction.* Not all stress is dysfunctional, and it typically does not last forever. While it might feel like we are endorsing where people are at the start, we do so as a means of bringing them into new realities through their role on a larger team. Acknowledging where people are in the moment is the start, not the destination.

2. *Showing empathy at work is a waste of time and money.* This can certainly feel true in the short term when, say, a manager is taking time away from a specific task to hear and understand the stress and pain that a team member suffers. But in the long term, empathy increases belonging, which creates an environment for greater productivity, not less. Taking the time to understand the pain of current team members is ultimately less expensive and time consuming than hiring someone else with presumably fewer needs.

3. *Entering into the lives of others is depressing.* It can be difficult to enter into stressful situations and stories that are not our own, especially when we have not been through similar pain ourselves. But Brené Brown suggests, "Empathy is a way to connect to the emotion another person is experiencing; it doesn't require that we have experienced the same situation they are

going through."[12] We can add to this that empathy does not require that we take on the stress of others, simply that we hear, acknowledge, and strive to understand. Being a light in someone's darkness does not have to dim your light.

4. *Weak people who need this level of care should not be working.* If this were the case, it's likely that none of us would be equipped to serve in organizations at various points in our lives! Just because someone is dealing with stress does not mean they are incapable of working. In cases where this really is true and someone's stress or pain is sincerely keeping them from doing the job, there are numerous health resources that can help both the staff member and the organization to get the additional support they need (some of these include the Society for Human Resource Management, local and national Employee Assistance Programs, or employer/employee health insurance benefits).

5. *We shouldn't have to change the organization to accommodate a small group of hurting people.* The assumption that most people at work are stress-, pain-, and trauma-free while only a handful are not is simply not true. Stress and painful experiences are present in every person and in every generation. When we adjust to accommodate those who are most affected by stress and painful realities, we make the organization better for everyone, regardless of what they may be experiencing in life.

6. *The only people who need this level of empathy are women, young people, and minorities.* Every single one of us can be affected by the realities of stress, trauma, and pain, regardless of our gender, age, or ethnicity. To blindly assume that White people or men or older people do not experience stress is to miss an opportunity to demonstrate Christlike empathy for others. While some stressors may affect us differently and some groups may be subject to greater amounts of systemic stress, our ability to tend to the needs of all people will be critical to organizational success.

7. *The workplace is not a church.* As church attendance continues to decrease in America and Christians become less affiliated with religious institutions, it is very likely that the workplace might be one of the few places where people can feel the love of God. No, the workplace is not the place for Communion, Eucharist, baptism, or other sacraments. We are not obligated to keep people at work in the way that we would fight to keep them in our religious communities. But the calling to lead with empathy and compassion is not limited to the pulpit and the pews. This calling should permeate our lives, causing our teams and organizations to be transformed by the light and life of Christ, regardless of where we work.

We can no longer afford to see leadership apart from those we lead. Given all that people have gone through and all that now affects each generation, the only way we can lead well now is by entering into the stress and pain of others with redemption, compassion, and grace. Redemptive leadership takes time to understand where people are in order to bring them to where they can be with empathy and love. In the words of practical theologian Rodney Cooper, "Redemptive leadership suggests that God does not use us *in spite* of who we are. He uses us *because* of who we are."[13] When we make spaces within our leadership styles and organizations to enter into the stress affecting others, we reinforce this beautiful invitation to join where God is working (John 5:17, 19-20). The incarnation proves that we are loved, seen, known, and heard not in spite of who we are but because of who we are as precious and valuable children of God.

2

TRIUMPHALISM, TRAUMA, AND THE AMERICAN CHURCH

EVERY AMERICAN IS A WINNER

There is an interesting debate in American child development on whether or not every child should receive an award. There are some who argue that everyone should get some type of award to encourage confidence and send the message that we are all special, no matter who comes in first. Life is hard, and sometimes just showing up and being present deserves a prize. Meanwhile, there are others who say that giving awards to everyone as children creates a sense of entitlement in adulthood. We stop striving for first place and expect to be awarded for mediocre participation in life. While both views have compelling arguments, what is common in both is the idea that praise and reward are important parts of the American experience. We want to be praised, whether for winning or participating. We want to be recognized, whether for being the best or simply having the best smile. By the time we become adults, we want to have a trophy wall that sings our praises so that everyone will know that our lives are special. We want to believe that we are not only special but, in some cases, more important than people beneath us. It makes us feel good to know that we have something that others do not. Even if we received a participation ribbon for a sport we lost, we pride ourselves in knowing that we at least tried.

This hunger for winning and reward is steeped into almost every area of American life. We don't just want any car; we want the best car. We don't strive for just any job; we want the best job. We don't even want to settle for decent sleep on an average mattress. No, we want the best sleep we can afford on the best mattress we can find. Why? Because we are winners who deserve the best that life can offer. In the triumphant exceptionalism of the American dream, only the strong survive, and the weak are cast aside. We are quick to vote people off the proverbial island and to cast lots for the ones we will name as America's best. We crave the kinds of competitions that will weed out the losers and reveal the victorious ones who made it through to the final round. While we may grieve for those who don't make it, we secretly see ourselves alongside those who do, cheering and screaming and chanting, "WE ARE THE CHAMPIONS!"

This winning attitude has deep roots that have been nurtured by generations of men and women who have championed our exceptionalism. Dating all the way back to the American Revolution, we have subtly accepted and reinforced ideas that America is superior to other nations and that no one else can match our strength and power. Alexis de Tocqueville introduced this concept in observations in 1840, stating, "The position of the Americans is therefore quite exceptional and it may be believed that no democratic people will ever be placed in a similar one."[1] From that time until now, our businesses and institutions have operated with a posture of superiority, believing that de Tocqueville's words are indeed our truth. Our values are superior to the values of others. Our democracy and politics are better than those in other countries. Whenever there is a sense that some other country may be doing better in some way than we are, we use that as competitive fuel to drive us to being the best that we believe ourselves to be. We pride ourselves on being the world's superpower and work hard to instill that reality into everything we do.

This history of exceptionalism was further reinforced through war and wealth. While seeds of American triumphalism were planted in our country's founding in 1776, they took root at the end of the Cold War with the collapse of the Soviet Union.[2] This victory confirmed America's superiority over other nations and positioned us at the forefront of global military prowess. We added wealth to that equation, becoming the richest country, per capita, in the world by 1890 and carrying that title into the present day.[3] When you bundle this history of exceptionalism, triumphalism, and victory into one story, you get a sense of the American ethos that permeates our institutions and ways of life. We all want a trophy because we know that, historically, we've earned it.

To be clear, we did not "woo" our way to the top or use superficial charisma to nudge other nations aside. Triumphalism in America exists because we have, indeed, been triumphant. The wars we've won were not just because we had nothing better to do. We have achieved victory because we fought with and on behalf of others. Our success has been earned by the blood and sacrifices of millions of families committed to protecting our country. American exceptionalism exists because, by God's grace, we are truly an exceptional nation. Believing that we are who God has allowed us to be is a gift that should not be taken lightly, especially when you consider the implications. For example, our national identity affects other nations globally, and we must own the responsibility of our global footprint. We own the fact that other countries look to the United States for everything from asylum to cultural trends, and that is not because we have been defeated. We are regarded as such due to our triumphant presence on the world stage, for better or worse. Yes, there are tremendous benefits to being considered a superpower on the global scene, and we should bear this honor with humility and without shame. But what happens when triumphalism and exceptionalism merge with the narrative of faith? While the benefits can be tempting, the results can be catastrophic for the church, for faith-based leaders, and for those we serve.

THE TRIUMPHANT CHURCH

"God gave us victory over the Brits. He gave us victory over the Indian. God gave us power to colonize the savage and to make a better life for the slave. Surely God is on our side!"

"God gave us victory over slavery. He gave us victory over Jim Crow and systematic injustice. God gave us power to fight for our rights and to win against those who tried to keep us down. Surely God is on our side!"

"God gave us victory over poverty and lack. He gave us victory over sickness and death. God has given us power to build wealth and strength to live in prosperity. Surely God is on our side!"

I remember hearing variations of these statements in three separate settings in one week. The first was spoken in a predominantly White setting with a faith-based interpretation of American history to empower business leaders. The second was a predominantly Black setting where a preacher encouraged Christian activists to persevere. The third was a multicultural, multilingual setting where participants were invited to support a global charity for children. Each group of listeners seemed to require something different to inspire action. All three contexts connected faith to victory, seeking to prove that God was with them, perhaps more than he was with others. Whether they knew it or not, they tapped into exceptionalism to appease the human need to feel special, unique, and chosen. They moved the crowds with reminders of what they believed God had already done to inspire faith in what God might do again.

While each narrative was different, some bearing more truths than others, each carried the same thread of triumph stemming from the presence of God on our side.

In some cases, this is true. The omnipresence of God gives all of us the ability to claim God "by our side" at all times and in all situations. But does God's presence with us validate our actions and experiences? Absolutely not! God is faithful to the promise to never leave us but clear in the expectation that we "act justly . . . love mercy and . . . walk humbly with your God" (Deuteronomy 31:6; Micah 6:8). In the first setting, this means acknowledging where we went wrong to make room for God to help us get it right. In the second setting, this means uplifting the communal success of the past to empower individual responsibility and accountability for the present. In the third setting, this requires honoring God's presence with us in times of abundance and times of lack, in health and in sickness, knowing that God's blessings are not limited to the mountain tops alone, but can be visible in the valleys of life as well.

The messages I heard in each setting were the same ones that are often repeated in churches across America each week. The narrative of triumphalism transcends natural divisions, affecting each of us in different ways. Whether we have triumphed because of the height of our success or we have triumphed because of the depth of our despair, our Christian narrative is still the same: we are those who have overcome. Regardless of our context, we can honestly declare that, in Christ, we have truly triumphed. In him, we are truly victorious, and that is a good thing. No one wants to follow a failed God. No one wants to belong to a losing church. Who wants to be affiliated with a faith of rejects whose narrative is that of defeat? No one does, and faith in Christ helps to uplift the downtrodden and give hope to the hopeless. Yet, a careful autopsy of triumph reveals that victory generally comes at the end of a series of failures. Triumph is part of the biblical narrative, but it is not the only part. And the resurrection gloat does not come without the crucifixion groan. Yes, we are winners in Christ, but the way that we win is by dying.

While triumphalism invites us to lean into resurrection, trauma invites us to lean into the cross. Yet what we hear in our churches is often a clear depiction of resurrection glory that somewhat or completely ignores the shame of crucifixion. And let's be honest: a message of winning is easier to communicate because it's softer for our ears to hear and for our minds to digest. Our society reinforces the Darwinian idea of the survival of the fittest, so it's only natural for us to want victory as a means of survival. The stresses of life make us hanker for a happy ending, and the resurrection story gives us just that. Our challenges and difficulties already make us feel like we're losing, so we need the triumphant Savior to bring us through. We have enough bad news all around, so why not use faith as the supplemental drug to get us through to the other side?

Here's the issue: while victorious faith and resurrection power are true and valuable, they cannot come at the expense of the cross.

The crux of our faith rests not only in the reality of the risen Savior but also in the trauma of his crucifixion and death. Some people live this reality more than others. Those who face socioeconomic and material challenges, working multiple jobs just to put food on the table, find comfort in the reality of the cross. Those whose parents fought through societal and national injustice just to survive find purpose in the power of the cross. In my own family, echoes of "we shall overcome" flow through the veins of each generation, pushing us to go just a little farther, reach just a little higher, and live more successfully than the generation before. If the stress and shame of the cross were unnecessary, we would have never seen the wounds on Christ's resurrected body (John 20:27). But instead, God chose to raise Jesus from the dead, wounds visible, so that we would know that his trauma was for our triumph and, therefore, our trauma can be redeemed through him. In Christ, we see the truth of victory: that while there is no crown without a cross, every cross can be redeemed by God's crown.

TRIUMPH AND TRAUMA IN THEOLOGICAL TENSION

We read in Revelation 5:6, "Then I saw a Lamb, looking as if it had been slain, standing at the center of the throne, encircled by the four living creatures and the elders."

Dr. Brian Blount describes the book of Revelation like a Quentin Tarantino movie.[4] Like *Pulp Fiction*, *Django Unchained*, or *Kill Bill*, the book is filled with gory and difficult images described in almost glorious and poetic fashion. And just like these movies, Blount suggests that it is not the content of the book that matters but the plot. In chapter five, this revelation is specifically linked to the opening of a scroll that scholars say holds the answers to all of the questions that have ever been asked, are being asked, and will ever be asked for all of humanity. It holds so many secrets that it is written on both sides, which is rare for a scroll, and it is sealed with not one or two seals but with seven. While we might find comfort in knowing that this scroll was in God's hand, the plot thickens and tension builds when the angel calls out, "Who is worthy to break the seals and open the scroll?" (Revelation 5:2).

With oppression and fear lurking behind him and the answers to the future waiting, unopened in front of him, John began to weep. He wept and wept until an elder appeared in the vision and consoled him saying, "Do not weep! See, the Lion of the tribe of Judah, the Root of David, has triumphed. He is able to open the scroll and its seven seals" (Revelation 5:5). As if watching a movie, we look around the scene and wait with anticipation for a brave lion to enter. We are waiting for Aslan to enter as he did in the Chronicles of Narnia. We are waiting for Mufasa to enter with strength and power as he mounted the cliff overlooking his tribe in *The Lion King*.

But the Revelation plot thickens again, and instead of the entrance of the lion, we witness the entrance of the Lamb. And this is not just any lamb; this is a lamb that John said looked like it was slain, slaughtered, and executed.

In biblical tradition, the priests would slaughter the lamb by slitting its throat with a sharp knife, letting the blood drip on the altar, and then either burning the flesh or hanging it on a hook to be eaten later. This was a vivid and common image for the people of Israel because that saw it daily through the practice of the Tamid. This ritual sacrifice was made up of two daily offerings of an unblemished young lamb at the entrance of the tent of meeting, every morning and every night. It is referenced throughout the Old Testament because the blood of the lamb was a significant part of the covenant. It protected them from death in Exodus 12, made it possible for Moses to meet with God in Exodus 29, was required to please God in Numbers 28, was used as a sin offering in Leviticus 4, and is symbolic of innocent life in 2 Samuel 12. The elders spoke of a lion, but John saw the lion as a bloody, symbolic Lamb who was slain for our sins and crucified for our redemption. But it was this shedding of blood that made him worthy to open the scroll.

Furthermore, John didn't just see a lamb lying on the ground in a pool of its own blood. He said, "I saw a Lamb, looking as if it had been slain, standing . . ." (Revelation 5:6). Clearly, this was a miracle because slaughtered animals do not stand. When they are slaughtered, they go limp and weak because their strength has been drained. But in this conquering vision of the Lamb was slain and yet still standing. The symbolism of standing on two feet is reminiscent of power, authority, and resilience. The Lamb may have once been slain by death, but it now stood in victory.

These visible wounds on the standing Lamb reminded John that resurrection was an act of spiritual defiance. Being raised from the dead did not erase the trauma of crucifixion but redeemed it in a very physical and tactical way. As if that weren't enough, John also wrote that he saw the Lamb, looking as if it had been slain, standing at the center of the throne. Jesus was the only one who could open the scroll because he was the Lamb slain, standing, and centered. Going back to this movie-like vision, John didn't see a perfect Lamb but a bloody one. He didn't see a Lamb lying down, he saw him standing firm. And he didn't see the Lamb on the margins, blending in with the elders, or off to the side of the throne. John saw this bloodied, standing Lamb right in the center of the throne, surrounded by the elders and the angels.

The centrality of the slain yet standing Lamb is a perfect picture of the life of faith. Each element of this vision is necessary to help us navigate the tensions between triumph and trauma, life and death. While the world would suggest that you can have one without the other, this image illustrates, with crystal clarity, that a life in Christ is both/and. In Christ, we can be both slain and standing. In Jesus, we can live even as we die. Our faith in the Savior is what gives us grace to identify with those who suffer and with those who win at the same time. In truth, we are not called to simply identify with those who live in this sacred tension; we are called to *be* those who live out this tension in life. The slain, standing, and centered Lamb reminds us that real discipleship does not always look like victory.

Sometimes, it looks like defeat and loss. At times, following Jesus can look like trauma and tragedy, even though we know that it will not stay that way. When we take up our crosses, we do so knowing that our wounds will be for his glory, which should change the way we live and dramatically transform the way we lead.

RENEWED VALUE FOR CRUCIFIXION

While triumph and trauma are always at odds, they are the most volatile in the field of leadership. Triumphant leadership in the context of a stressed, burdened, and traumatized world can feel like a bull trampling through a fine porcelain and glass shop. It knows no weakness. It is unaware of how it affects fragile objects nearby. It never apologizes for antiques that have been broken and never stops to repair what has been damaged. The triumphant bull throws its weight in the direction of victory and sacrifices anything and anyone who might stand in the way. No matter how bad the damage might be, our longing for strength over weakness often causes us to select strong, callous bulls to lead us. They are the ones who have won the most awards, the ones who have garnered the greatest influence, the ones who are attractive enough and successful enough to cause others to follow. Triumphant leadership cares only about the highs and practically ignores the lows, believing that nothing can keep a strong person down. It teaches us that exceptional leaders are better than other people, and those who are perceived to be weak in any way can only be helped by someone stronger. American triumphalism produces leaders who want to win, believe they must win, and might even be willing to do whatever it takes to keep the status they think they deserve. But this vision of triumphant leadership is the opposite of what is called for by Christ. The standing, slain Lamb demands that leaders and those who want to stand at the center in victory must first be willing to die to anything that is not like him.

For pastors and church leaders, this is a necessary part of ministry. Andrew Purves underscores this truth, declaring, "Whether we minister with mediocre skill or with truckloads of competence, whether with small success or with much public acclaim, God brings us to the point where our reliance on what we can do is killed by God."[5] The same is true for leadership beyond the church. While triumphalism and exceptionalism are applauded by the world, humility and divine dependence are applauded by God. If we are going to lead well in the midst of those who are broken, we must learn to let crucifixion take root in our lives to lead us to grace-filled resurrection and hope. In other words, leadership is designed to kill you. But dying to the success of the world is the only way to truly lead like Christ. This is precisely what we will unpack in the next chapters.

It goes without saying that crucifixion is not easy. It is not natural, and even when we know that death is necessary, it is hardly ever desirable. If we are going to take this journey of leadership, we will need to be anchored in the power of God's Word. While there are many passages that will help us redefine and prepare for crucifixion in leadership, here are just a few to get you started:

1. *"Then he said to them all: 'Whoever wants to be my disciple must deny themselves and take up their cross daily and follow me'" (Luke 9:23).* The cross is required before the crown. What posture will you need to take on to carry your cross?

2. *"For through the law I died to the law so that I might live for God" (Galatians 2:19).* Dying to the world is necessary to live for God. What do you anticipate will be your greatest obstacles in dying to the world?

3. *"For you died, and your life is now hidden with Christ in God" (Colossians 3:3).* Take comfort in knowing that crucifixion leads to deeper intimacy with Christ in God. Who else can come alongside you as you strive to follow Christ in this new way?

4. *"For to me, to live is Christ and to die is gain" (Philippians 1:21).* While crucifixion can feel like loss, Christ reminds us that we have so much to gain. How can you stay focused on what is gained without being burdened by what is lost?

5. *"We were therefore buried with him through baptism into death in order that, just as Christ was raised from the dead through the glory of the Father, we too may live a new life" (Romans 6:4).* Crucifixion promises new life. What do you anticipate will be your joy in taking on a new life of leadership?

6. *"And if the Spirit of him who raised Jesus from the dead is living in you, he who raised Christ from the dead will also give life to your mortal bodies because of his Spirit who lives*

in you" (Romans 8:11). Crucifixion and resurrection are works of the Holy Spirit. How can you make room in your life to embrace this spiritual work?

7. *"This is how we know what love is: Jesus Christ laid down his life for us. And we ought to lay down our lives for our brothers and sisters" (1 John 3:16)*. Crucifixion is not only for us in relationship to God but also for us in relationship with each other. What do you need to believe about other people in order to lay down your life for them?

While there is much to be said about the role that triumph plays into our ability to survive, it cannot come at the expense of redemption through the cross. The only way that we can bring healing through our leadership is to lean into the cross. While the triumphalism of resurrection appeals to us all, it is the apparent failure of the cross that must ultimately define us. We are overcoming and victorious and successful not simply because Jesus rose, but specifically because he rose *from the dead*. Resurrection is powerful not simply because of the miracle of life, but specifically because of *life after death*. And it is this death, this trauma, this sorrow and pain that is the best connection we have to traumatized people.

PART 2

THE

PROGRESSION

3

CRUCIFYING POWER

*From Personal Control
to Complete Surrender*

*What makes power dangerous is how it's used.
Power over is driven by fear. Daring and transformative
leaders share power with, empower people to, and
inspire people to develop power within.*

BRENÉ BROWN

I have a love-hate relationship with power. I love it because I understand the challenges and frustrations that come from powerlessness and the need for power to transform our lives. No one should feel powerless to make decisions that affect their own safety or survival. Powerless leaders feel trapped and ineffective, incapable of making meaningful change. The times in my life when I felt powerless were times when I felt most weak and vulnerable. Without power and agency, we are forced to live at the whims of others, hoping that those with power will not wield it over us for evil. These experiences have caused me to fight for power and to believe in it as a necessary part of leadership. At the same time, I hate the effects that power can have on people. It drives good people to make horrible choices, often sacrificing common sense for self-centered visions of grandeur. Power tempts people to forget who they are and why they serve. It can be used to oppress and suppress what was intended to be freed and uplifted. But how can you hate something that you need in order to lead and live well? And what is the right balance, given the fact that variables for leadership (who you lead, what you're leading toward, the context in which you lead, etc.) seem to change with each season and are different depending on how much power you actually have?

It's helpful to first start with one central truth: God has given everyone some level of power, whether we choose to exercise it or not. By God's grace, each of us has power to bear witness to God, regardless of where we serve. In some cases, power shows up from the least likely people and places, demonstrating God's strength in weakness and God's presence with those most broken. In other cases, power shows up in the form of protest, pushing against power structures that attempt to keep others down. In many cases, power shows up within us, as we adapt to the places and times in which we serve. Whether our power is overt or subversive, whether in view or working behind the scenes, every one of us has God-given power, and we must understand what that means. If we want to lead and live well, it pays to know whether the power within must be built up or toned down, made visible or invisible, used in opposition to existing power or in support of it. And this is no easy task.

Perhaps this is why leadership specialists from every generation have spent their lives trying to find the perfect mix of power that strengthens the whole without weakening the individual parts. Too little power in life or leadership can leave people susceptible to abuse and mistreatment. Too much power carries a series of consequences, including excessive self-centeredness, disconnection from others, and a willingness to do whatever it takes to keep power. As much as some would rather not deal with power at all, we cannot lead without it. After all, power is arguably one of the most important aspects of leadership. The natural interconnectedness of leadership and power makes it difficult to see one without the other; the two go hand in hand. While it is possible to find a few instances of power without being a leader, it is virtually impossible to lead without power. Leaders need power to serve others well, to accomplish collective goals, and to guide those who follow. But, like many good things in life, too much of it used in the wrong way can be deadly. Like salt in water, power redefines and reshapes the look and feel of leadership, making it either an elixir or a poison to those who drink it.

It's likely you've had your own wrestling match with power as well. At its best, power has helped you to find your voice, understand your calling, and believe that change was possible in and through you. At its worst, power has probably tempted to consume you, hogging space in your life that used to be reserved for empathy, only to twist you into wanting more of it for yourself. It can be both a soothing balm and a tormenting bully. Power is both a compassionate coach and a demanding client. Leaning too far into either side of this love-hate relationship can not only hurt you but can significantly harm those around you as well. Because if there is one thing that has the greatest potential to injure traumatized, stressed, and broken people, it is the misuse of power in leadership.

DEFINING POWER

While power is often easy to recognize, it can be hard to clearly define. We can instinctively know when we and others are operating with power without always knowing what kind of power is at work. In the 1950s, John French and Bertram Raven came up with five social bases of power and added a sixth in later years.[1] These six social bases of power can help us define what power looks like and identify how to use it for good. They are as follows:

1. *Legitimate power.* Often associated with a person's hierarchy, legitimate power comes with a specific role or title that legalizes his or her authority. CEOs, senior pastors, C-suite executives, directors, managers, supervisors, and the like all have legitimate power by virtue of their titles and their position of authority over others.

2. *Reward power.* This power base stems from one's ability to stimulate behavior based on relevant prizes and

penalties. This type of power often requires some level of authority over money or the employment of others to truly be effective, which tends to imply a higher role within the organization.

3. *Coercive power.* Coercive power is the only negative social power base named by French and Raven because of its ability to force people into submission to ideas or tasks they may not believe in. Coercion requires some needed or desired outcome to be used against those who do not comply (e.g., money, promotion, influence).

4. *Expert power.* Expertise is a power based on what a person knows or has experienced beyond others. As an expert in a particular field of interest, they are perceived as people who have earned the right to speak and be heard, regardless of their specific role on the team.

5. *Referent power.* Referent power is often linked with some level of respect or admiration. It can accompany tenure, age, expertise, or anything else that causes others to defer to them out of reverence or even fear. People often feel a connection to those with referent power and can be persuaded by them, regardless of the role they occupy in the organizational structure.

6. *Informational power.* The idea that "data is king" drives some leaders to lean into the informational power base to achieve results. This power base is dependent not on organizational position but on information that can inform leadership decisions. People with

informational power can sway a decision with "facts" from empirical evidence or research that others need.

These six social bases allow us to define and understand how power can be used, for good and for evil, in various settings in our lives. They help us see how various powers can flow into each other, allowing some people to operate out of multiple power bases at one time. For example, a CEO with clear budget analytics can have legitimate and informational power at the same time. A beloved manager with long tenure who promises a party when the team succeeds can operate with referent and reward power at the same time.

While these social bases of power are comprehensive, there may be one area that French and Raven overlooked: the social base of cultural privilege. Privilege is defined as "unearned power, benefits, advantages, access and/or opportunities that exist for members of the dominant group(s) in society."[2] Privilege complicates power because those of the privileged group are afforded societal power over others, often without being aware of the power they've been granted. Having this cultural privilege means that you are seen as someone with power that comes as your birthright, whether you choose to acknowledge that power or not. In American society, this privilege is most often afforded people in one or more of the following social groups:

- White people
- able-bodied people
- heterosexuals

- men
- Christians
- middle or owning class people
- middle-aged people
- English-speaking people[3]

Unlike power, which is often seen and understood by multiple people within an organization, privilege can go unseen and unnamed. It tends to complicate power structures because those who possess it are typically unaware of it. Once identified, privileged groups can feel offended, adding greater complication to power with the idea that those of lesser privilege can see what those of greater privilege can deny. The same is true in global and multicultural contexts. In some African contexts, select tribes have greater privilege over others. In some Indian contexts, certain castes have legal privilege over those "beneath" them. Wherever you go, you'll find that there are privileges and systems at work to ensure that some people remain at the top while others stay at the bottom.

Cultural privilege can make other social bases of power difficult or even irrelevant when it comes to leadership. For example, people with no or low privilege who step into legitimate power can still feel powerless. This is what can happen when a young woman is promoted to lead a team of older men. Although she has legitimate power by way of her position, she can feel invalidated by the privilege that society gives to the older men on her team. This is worsened if she does not have support from someone above her or an ally in someone alongside or reporting to her with courage to reinforce her role as the highest power at play. At the same time, persons with high privilege can serve in positions of low power and still feel powerful. Such is the case when a person of a preferred tribe serves on a team full of people from a perceived lower tribe. Even with a low seat at the table, privilege is still afforded to the person of the preferred tribe, giving them referent power to be heard each time they speak. This can be worsened if someone within the organization is not willing to establish the hierarchy of power that minimizes culture and accentuates structural roles.

Privilege becomes even more complicated in the context of leadership in faith-based organizations. For example, when the senior leader is of the dominant cultural class, gender, or race in the church and believes that he or she is the only one who can or should hear from God, the power dynamics can easily be exploited. Such is the case when charismatic religious cult leaders, often from a position of privilege, manipulate followers of lower classes or social categories into acts that have nothing to do with God.

While each of these social bases of power and privilege can be extremely complicated, they can also be used for good. Again, our general premise is that God has given everyone some degree of power, regardless of their race, class, wealth, or any other area of social standing. This means that we must recognize the power bases and privilege from which we operate in order to serve God well. No matter what level of leadership you've been given, the task is to identify that power, walk in that power, and use that power for the glory of God and the good of others. Since this is the case, the question cannot be, Who has power? but rather, What can I do with the power I have?

In any given circumstance, power can be wielded for good or for evil, to help or to hurt, to build up or to tear down, whether from an earned social base or from unearned privilege. While each power base carries its own distinctive dark side, the one thing they all have in common is the dark side of the self. The greatest temptation in leadership is to focus on oneself at the expense of those we lead. Therefore, when power turns in on itself, we can expect nothing less than implosion of selfishness that results in a painful explosion against innocent bystanders. Powerful people can easily become selfish, hoarding power for themselves or using power to create their own platforms without any regard for others. For this reason, we must wrestle with power at play in our lives, not simply because of how it affects us but especially because of how it affects others.

Left unchecked, power can give us an overinflated sense of ourselves, causing us to ignore people around us in pursuit of our own gain. It can cause us to think that the world, our organizations, and the people around us exist for us and that we can use them for our own glory. When we operate in this way, even short-term gains can lead to long-term regret with a trail of blood from the victims we've massacred along the way. Therefore, if we are going to lead suffering people in hope-filled ways, earthly power and privilege must be crucified so that God's power and grace may be resurrected in us. It does not need to be redeemed by us; it must be redeemed by God. Redemption implies that we buy it back and regain control of that which is out of our control. This, too, is the deceptive nature of power that leads people to believe that they have everything (and everyone) within their control. When we understand the truth that nothing and no one is truly within our control, we will see that the only way to crucify power is by restoring it back to the One who gave it in the first place. In doing so, we will find that what is resurrected in its place is a sense of divinely driven power that brings healing to our brokenness and flows through us to bring that same healing to others as well.

RESTORING POWER

While there are various forms of power in the world, the truest sense of power comes from God. If we were to conduct a word study, we'd find more than 260 Hebrew references and more than 150 references in the Greek that describe divine power.[4] The most common New Testament mentions to God's power are *dynamis* (miraculous), *exousia* (authority), and *kratos* (strength). Each of these translations speak to a supernatural power and might that only come from God. When this divine power is evident through humanity, it is for the purposes of glorifying the source, not the vessel. For example, when Luke tells the story of Jesus giving Holy Spirit *dynamis* to his disciples in Acts 1:8, it is specifically given so they can be witnesses of God throughout the earth. Likewise, when Jesus sent out the Twelve with *exousia* to drive out demons in Mark 3:15, it was to demonstrate God's authority over darkness, not their own. When Paul admonishes the church in Ephesus to be strong in the Lord and in his *kratos*, he is reminding them that their might must be rooted in the divine.

So, how can we restore back to God what has been entrusted to us for life and leadership? For this, we look to Jesus as the perfect example of divine power. Jesus was constantly aware of his power and communicated this regularly to those he served. He repeatedly told the disciples that his mission and power came from God. His words were not his own (John 12:50). His will was not his own (John 5:19). His works were not his own (John 14:10). Literally, everything Jesus said, desired, and did came from God.

Even when he wanted something different for himself, as he did in the Garden of Gethsemane, he was willing to lay his power down for the will of the Father. In Luke 22:42, Jesus prayed for his own will, that the cup of sorrow and death would pass him, but surrendered his will to God stating, "Yet not my will, but yours be done." This simple yet stunning statement from Christ became the ultimate declaration of the crucifixion that was soon to come. Dying was not his will but, knowing that this was the only way to secure our salvation, he surrendered to God's will against his own. In an intimate moment of prayer that was overheard by the exhausted, overwhelmed disciples, Jesus clarified once more that any power he had was surrendered to God. He had power to walk away. He had power to desire a different outcome. Jesus even had power to keep the disciples awake and ready to fight! But none of his power mattered in the presence of the omnipotent Father. What mattered most to Jesus was the glory of the Father, and he was willing to do whatever it took, even taking on sin on the cross, to ensure that God alone received glory. And the beauty of this deliberate act of surrender and submission is that God glorified Jesus as Jesus glorified the Father (John 17:1).

God has given us power and all power comes from God! Jesus demonstrates that we can maximize this power for God's glory by crucifying it. The way we crucify power is by acknowledging and surrendering our words, our will, and our works to Jesus who surrenders it all to God. In the mysterious cycle of the Trinity, we are empowered by the Holy Spirit to recognize and surrender our power to Jesus, who is completely surrendered and submitted to God as Father, who gives us divine power through the Spirit to glorify the Godhead. In other words, the only way we can operate in this triune power (from God as Father, Son, and Holy Spirit) is to surrender and restore that power back to the Godhead. When we try to keep power that was given to us by God and not return it to God for God's glory, we attempt to take ownership over what was not ours in the first place. We start to claim God's success as our own and can subtly take God's glory for ourselves. What's worse is when we try to hoard power for ourselves, refusing to restore it to God or to share it with others. This is where the selfish implosion begins and power that was meant to build us and others up becomes the very thing that tears us and others down.

In a healthy distribution of power, we receive power from God and others, restore it back to God, and share whatever power we have from whatever position we hold with others around us (see fig. 1). This is what happens when leaders with positional power use their platforms to elevate those working behind the scenes. It's what happens when a pastor with referent power makes room for people with lesser privilege to be heard. By contrast, in an unhealthy distribution of power, we receive power from God, refusing to recognize the source or the fact that God has given others power as well, and use it to make ourselves more powerful by demeaning and discouraging others. Leaders with unhealthy views of power can easily rob others of their power and rob glory from God. This is what happens when leaders with informational power limit access to information to discourage others from finding answers beyond them. It's what happens when those with expert power operate as if they are the only experts in every area by tearing down any ideas that did not originate with them. While they may feel like they are building their own power and elevating themselves over the people they serve, they are, in effect, chipping away at God's desire for empowered community and gradually wearing people down. Instead of creating a dynamic power engine of an organization that can advance mission and vision, they create a splintered engine that doesn't have enough power in any one area to make anything meaningful happen (see fig. 2).

Figure 1. Healthy distribution of leadership power: from God, to God, from others to others

Figure 2. Unhealthy distribution of leadership power: from God, to us, for us to restrain others

EXCHANGING OUR POWER FOR GOD'S

Whenever Christian leaders recognize the source of their power (restoring it to God) and then give it away (empowering others), they tap into a triune power with divine force that is unlike anything in this world. After all, eternal impact can only come from the power and will of God. For leaders seeking to make this kind of lasting impact, it will require a regular, intentional process of restoring and giving and repurposing power for God's glory and not our own. Regardless of the context in which we serve, the resurrection of divine power can only come from the crucifixion of human power as we once perceived it. Following the model of Jesus, this involves a regular process of identifying our power bases and then surrendering our words, our will, and our works in ways that honor God and empower others.

Identify your power base. You cannot surrender what you have not acknowledged. In the same way that Jesus was constantly aware of his power, you and I must be aware of the power and privilege we want to surrender to God. In some cases, this power is clear because it is legitimate or expert or referent power. In these cases, we must offer our roles, our expertise, and our revered positions to the Lord. We can ask God to help us navigate these areas of clear power in ways that give honor and glory back to him and extend power to those who need it most.

In other cases, the power we have may not be as clear, especially when affected by privilege or when the dark side of power dominates our personalities. These are the times when we must lean on the perspectives of others to tell us how they experience power from us. No matter what we hear, the next step is to surrender that power and privilege to God, believing that God will transform for healing what may have been previously used for harm. We can confess that we are not always aware of the power at work in our lives and ask God to reveal it for his glory and for the good of those we serve. In moments when we feel sincerely powerless, either because of our cultural or organizational position or because of an injustice that has robbed us of the power God has provided, our task is to believe that what God has instilled cannot be extinguished by humanity. If God has given everyone power, then no one but God can take it away.

Surrendered words. It's often been stated that "he who controls the narrative controls the people." This quote underscores the power of words to affect what people believe and how they behave. We see this at work in the most abusive ways in spiritual communities and faith-based organizations where faith can be easily manipulated to control others. Often gifted with great charisma, leaders in these contexts can frame a narrative that causes people to see themselves over and against the world. These leaders create narratives of fear and use words of victimization and warfare to effectively sway the rationality of their followers. By the power of their words, they can convince people to put their faith in a person either as an extension of or a replacement for God. They base their empowerment on the ability to make missionaries of their followers, convincing them to get others to believe the words they preach. Sadly, this abuse of power through words is not only limited to unhealthy faith leaders. We see words used to control others in politics, in profit industries, in education, and even in the medical field. The power of words has long been woven into the fabric of history, and people have used words to enslave, oppress, discourage, and suppress.

However, when a leader's words are surrendered to God, we can see the exact opposite take root. Like sports coaches or cheerleaders, these leaders can find ways to inspire and encourage teams that win, even when the odds are against them. With words that are rooted in God's Word, leaders can remind their teams that their worth and meaning go far beyond any one project or task. They can rejuvenate those who may be downtrodden and create a narrative of shared success that keeps people going through whatever comes their way. While the journey of surrendering our words to God will not be easy, it is possible when we make the following exchanges:

In private planning: *God, I don't know what to say, but you will give me the words to say at the right time.*

In group meetings: *I am not afraid to retract words that were not helpful, reframe words that need to be restated, or amplify the voices of others who say it better.*

In personal conversation: *I will use my words to reflect to others what I hear and not only what I want to say.*

In conflict: *I will slow my words, using them sparingly and wisely to bring justice, restore relationship, and amplify God's truth over my own.*

Surrendered will. While surrendering our words may feel very tactical, surrendering our wills can feel very ethereal. It's easy to assess someone's views of power by what they say but much more difficult to assess power by what they will. When a leader lives with his or her will surrendered to God, they hold their own dreams and visions lightly. They are more prone to pivot when circumstances are leading them in a new direction, more likely to let go of plans they had that are no longer working, and more open to changes in the strategies they have set for the organization or the team. Surrendering the power of the will means recognizing that we are not the only ones who dream and we are certainly not the only ones who can make them happen. This is not to say that we do not have a will or dreams or visions for ourselves and others. On the contrary, Jesus demonstrates that a surrendered will includes the power to have a desire and still give permission to God to reshape or redirect that will according to his desires. In the journey of life and leadership, a surrendered will can look like this:

In private planning: *God, this is what I want, but please give us what you want.*

In group meetings: *I have a desired outcome, but I remain open to new directions that may come from the team.*

In personal conversation: *I will hold my desires loosely enough to be enhanced by others.*

In conflict: *I will not let my will keep me from understanding the will of others, even when we do not agree.*

Surrendered works. The most obvious display of power comes by what we do. By surrendering our works to God, we surrender both our successes and our failures to him. This means that while we do not need to take credit for every mistake or work that does not achieve what we intended, we also cannot take credit for our successes and the things that we did well. Surrendering our works allows us to do our part as if it depended on us but to trust God's power through us since it ultimately depends on him. This level of surrender is often difficult, especially when it comes to finding balance between the two extremes. On one hand, we can overly absorb the praise from good works, believing that we were responsible for our own victory. On the other hand, we can overly deflect praise, telling people that we had nothing to do with anything good as a means of honoring God. But, by tapping into God's power, we can experience his work through us to be better and stronger than anything we could have done by ourselves; it cements the fact that he should get the glory. As challenging as it may be, the deliberate act of surrendering our works to God is a necessary part of remembering who is truly in control. This level of surrender can show up like this:

In private planning: *God, please give me power to do this work and give you the glory from anything that comes from it.*

In group meetings: *When we work together to make this happen, we will see God do more through us than we could imagine by ourselves.*

In personal conversation: *I will not let my works define me or hog successful outcomes as if they belong to me alone.*

In conflict: *I will strive to ensure that the works of my hands measure up to the intentions of my heart.*

The journey to surrender is just that: a journey. It will not happen overnight. The results may not be instantaneous. The impact may not be immediately felt. It may not be easy for us, as it was not easy for Jesus. But the cumulative effect of transformational power over time is that those burdened and traumatized by the ways of the world will find safety in God's power through us without fear of power being used against them. With perseverance, we can lead with power to heal the brokenhearted and empower those who feel weak. No, this journey will not be easy, but over time, we will find that this power exchange is absolutely worth it.

4

CRUCIFYING EGO

*From Self-Centeredness
to Divine Love*

EGOMANIA

The sign over the door of the marketing department proudly boasted, "No Logos, No Egos!" They'd spent the last five years at the missional technology company building a white label app for churches and Christian organizations to weave seamlessly into their existing systems. The goal of the app was to make church administration easier, and they'd succeeded in building something that actually worked. But the founder did not want his company to be prideful or arrogant. He worked hard to infuse a deep sense of humility among the team, one that included inconspicuous logos and practically nonexistent egos. To him, the best way to honor God was by not being seen or heard in any way. His strategy worked well for organizations who knew of him and wanted to add their own logos to the technology. But to the sales team, this was the one way to ensure the ultimate death of the company. If people were using their products but no one else knew who they were, how would they survive? In a world full of skeptics, who would believe that they didn't want any credit for themselves?

While the founder was proud of their position, the rest of the team worried that what appeared to be "market humility" would prove to be "market invisibility" in just a matter of time. They urged the founder to get in front of the business marketing and become more of the face for the public to experience the product. As a likable, charismatic figure with gifts of speaking in public, it made sense to them that he would be more in front. But his commitment to leaving egos behind meant staying in the shadows, denying his involvement in public promotion, and encouraging team members to "let the product speak for itself." After another four years of unsuccessfully trying to get new partners on board, the company was forced to close its doors.

Across the street was a large church who employed the app. They readily displayed their logo, their church slogan, and their color-themed template on the features so that everyone using it knew who they were. Their billboard just a few blocks away featured prominently for miles a picture of the pastor and a QR code to their website. At the pastor's request, the church PR team made sure that the pastor and key staff members were regularly featured on the local news and had consistent presence on radio and television stations. They provided area homeless shelters and food banks with customized water bottles to magnify the brand and regularly invited families to church through community reading programs and afterschool activities. The pastor was certain that this strategy was the only way to grow the church. His motto was clear: advertise to evangelize.

He was confident that people only came to church to hear the preaching and the music, so he took strides to improve his personal appeal and to make himself visible on their music albums and playlists each year. While the leader relished this approach, the staff members and lay leaders recoiled. They worried that commercial advertising would eventually be perceived as "fake news" and would only attract scrutiny instead of positive attention. They feared that the more people saw the church's public campaign, the less likely they would be to enter the doors. Furthermore, they were afraid to share with the pastor that his leadership and preaching style needed improvement. Sermons often went for seventy-five minutes, and his commitment to plastic surgeries started to make him look unreal. But any level of feedback was met with instant rebuke and with his normal explanation, "I am the brand." After several years of public presence, the pastor soon succumbed to moral failure in the eyes of the church and was asked to step down. Six months later, he started a new church with a new personal look and organizational marketing plan to attract members.

This is a classic tale of two simultaneous realities, both doomed to fail in different ways. In one story, an organization underestimated the importance of ego, and in the other, they overestimated how much ego played into their identity. Both obsessed over their public images in ways that would eventually lead to irrelevance, but only one would be perceived as successful to society. While the intentions of humility were valid in the tech leader, the arrogance of the pastor is more likely to be the one seen and celebrated by others. Regardless of whether other people or organizations would be willing to go to the same lengths of boasting for the same reasons, no one could argue with the numbers. The church grew in attendance, even when the pastor went to great lengths to make himself synonymous with the brand. The tech company, on the other hand, lost clients, even when the leader did everything he could to promote others over himself. One failed for not thinking enough of himself and the organization he represented, while the other failed for thinking too much about them. Sadly, society tends to applaud the latter.

EGO . . . IT'S COMPLICATED

Before we jump on our bandwagons of either bashing or affirming egos, it's important to understand just how complex and confusing the concept of ego can be. In some ways, it operates like a patchwork quilt with a combination of psychological, philosophical, spiritual, and practical meanings. On the simplest level, *ego* is the Latin word for "I." Ego is you and how you perceive yourself over and against the world around you. Some credit the earliest uses of *ego* in psychology to Freud's translated work.

Ego was a translation of what Freud, writing in German, called "das Ich"—literally "the I." In essence, Freud was referring to that conscious, decision-making part of you that you regard as "I," as when you say "I dislike my mother" or "I decided to change jobs" or "I dreamt that my house was on fire last night." That is your I, your ego.[1]

In this sense, the ego is the multifaceted part of you that influences your thoughts, emotions, and actions. According to modern philosophy, ego and egoism can be understood as the normal pursuit of one's own welfare.[2] It is expected that each of us should do what it takes for our own survival. But ego becomes a challenge when we consider this pursuit in light of our ethical, moral, and social understandings and obligations. For Christians, these obligations are based in Scripture, providing details on how we should live in relationship with the world. In business, the ego thrives when survival is linked to personal gains and profits that might also benefit the organization. Whether in psychology or philosophy, whether in business or in ministry, the ego is the self and the self is complicated, especially when we consider the ego that is necessary for thriving in leadership.

When it comes to the workplace, we are often quick to define ego by its negative extremes as it shows up in egotistical, egocentric, and egomaniacal leaders. This is to be expected as some experts suggest that the world is becoming increasingly more self-absorbed.[3] Globally, the more independent we become, the more self-reliant and self-centered we become. As we stop depending on other people and become more detached from others, we begin to think that no one else matters more than ourselves. This gradual shift toward hyper-individualism can subtly become a shift toward thinking that the world, and everyone in it, revolves around us. This thinking affects everything, from how we operate in relationships to how we raise our children, consciously and unconsciously training them to see themselves as the center of the picture, the center of the family, and even the center of life with friends. When you add the self-focused dimensions of social media, it's no wonder that narcissism continues to rise. For some, your ego is your brand, which should be elevated and promoted at all times and in every possible way. Why be present for the moment when you can post a video or a picture for others to see as well? Why use a flawed, natural view of yourself when you can use filters to look your absolute best? As societies become increasingly selfish, we also become increasingly fatigued with overinflated egos that suck the energy from every room.

Another complicating factor of defining ego is that of our social and cultural perspectives. Some specialists call these our worldviews: "A worldview is a collection of attitudes, values, stories and expectations about the world around us, which inform our every thought and action."[4] By this definition, worldviews also affect how we see ourselves and how we define the ego. In missiology and Christian sociology, there are said to be at least three core worldviews: honor/shame, guilt/innocence, and fear/power.[5] Each one carries its own values and therefore its own definitions of the self. For example, ego is frowned on in cultures built around honor and shame. In the case of some Eastern cultures where community is prized, it's not right to talk about ego, let alone to define it, and having any sense of self-confidence or self-esteem is perceived as shameful and rude.

For contexts framed in guilt and innocence, as is the case of most Western cultures where individualism is highly valued, ego is more positively defined. In these cultures, the ego plays out in self-justification, always ready to defend its innocence in word, thought, and deed. In yet a third cultural context based on fear and power, ego is defined in relationship to dominance and vulnerability. In these cultures, the ego is defined in more spiritual terms and one's self-esteem comes from what's happening in the spirit realms around them. Confidence, for instance, can come from priestly blessings while low self-esteem could be the result of a curse or representative of favor withdrawn from the ancestors. Because of such drastic differences in cultural perspectives, it's impossible to take a one-size-fits-all approach to defining or balancing ego. Some cultures will need to be encouraged to believe more in themselves while others may need to tone things down.

The complexity of ego continues when we factor in our personalities and gifts. According to the American Psychological Association, personality is defined as, "the enduring characteristics and behavior that comprise a person's unique adjustment to life, including major traits, interests, drives, values, self-concept, abilities, and emotional patterns."[6] The uniqueness of our personalities creates even more distinction between our understandings of ego. Psychologists and sociologists are so familiar with this aspect of self-perception that we have hundreds of personality tests to help us understand ourselves. From Myers-Briggs to the Enneagram, we attempt to define ourselves against the world so that we might understand how our egos can succeed alongside others. The challenge becomes determining how one's personality fits with one's gifting and cultural worldview. For example, an Enneagram 3 who feels constantly degraded by society may need to strengthen the ego to lead on the job while, perhaps, decreasing ego to function on a volunteer team at church. Concurrently, an ISTJ who feels regularly overlooked on her job may also need greater confidence and ego to succeed at work while potentially downplaying her ego when it comes to her marriage. While personality tests in both cases might suggest that they need to be "more humble" or that ego needs to be toned down, their complex realities would suggest that it really depends on where they are and how they need to show up in those spaces.

Because of these intricacies and the unique conceptualization of ego, it's fair to say there is no such thing as a common approach for all people. Being told to "be humble" or to simply "believe in yourself" does not seem to fit the bill for any wide group of people across demographic or cultural lines. So, how do we know how much is too much, especially when ego is so prominent in our lives and celebrated across vocations? What incentive do we have to minimize ego in cases when it's overinflated, knowing that a strong ego is necessary for leadership?

THE EGO EFFECT

If some level of ego is necessary to live, a slightly greater degree is necessary to lead. In this sense, I'm referring to the psychological, philosophical, normative sense of self. You have to believe in yourself in order to lead others. You cannot lead an organization unless you actually think you'll be successful. And this is where ego starts to become even more complex because how much ego you need must be tempered by key, concurrent realities, the most important of which are the people you lead. Strong personalities often have stronger egos than they realize. The confidence they exude often makes people feel more insecure. While the effects of one's ego cannot always be controlled, understanding the role that personality plays in ego and leadership can make a difference in how we lead. For example, a leader with a big ego tends to be extremely self-centered. They push others with their own agendas, often ignoring or not caring about the effect this may have on the team. Extreme egos can cost organizations, causing them to lose internal and external trust, overall productivity, and team members who refuse to tolerate the toxicity of egocentrism. If it is true that "ego is the invisible line item on every company's profit and loss statement," then an overinflated ego is extremely costly for everyone involved.[7] Rather than taking the opportunity to imbue greater confidence and ego in the team, these types of leaders hoard it, extending a narrative that only the talented survive, the most talented of which is the leader himself or herself.

Conversely, leaders who struggle with a weak sense of themselves can also project big egos, but often out of their own insecurity. They lead by making others feel lower than themselves so that they can feel some level of higher importance. Insecure leaders are more likely to micromanage their teams out of fear that no one's work will measure up, which carries the risk of exposure for the leader. Hyacinth Guy, vice president of human resources at Caribbean Airlines, says,

> A micromanager is a person who probably has a poor self-image, so he or she doesn't believe they deserve to be where they are, and so thinks the same about the people they supervise. . . . So the constant checking and looking over employees' shoulders are really checks on their own ability to do the job. They don't believe in themselves, so they believe in no one else.[8]

Along with micromanaging, insecure leaders may also be susceptible to bullying and coercion of employees, creating a toxic environment that makes it nearly impossible for others to succeed. But for the leader with low self-esteem, it doesn't matter whether others succeed or not. What matters most is the self-justification of their own actions and the achievement of their own success.

Teams suffer in environments where the leader's ego is either too big or too small, namely because both extremes cause leaders to care more about themselves and their own well-being without concern for others. While some employees may tolerate the imbalance of ego in leaders for a season, the long-term impact on others may be incalculable. How leaders see themselves affects how team members see themselves, either as critical and valuable or as expendable and worthless. Once people on a team feel like their presence and contributions don't matter, it's only a matter of time before they respond to protect their own egos by checking out, quitting, retaliating, or worse.

EGO SUM DEUS—I AM GOD

Having an ego is a necessary, complicated reality for leadership, and for this reason, it must be crucified with Christ. This level of self-surrender may be the only way to truly understand how to balance the challenges and opportunities our egos present. Jesus models for us a way of being and understanding ego that captures the challenges and nuances of thinking either too much or too little of ourselves. As fully God and fully man, Jesus lived in the tensions of worldviews, personalities, cultures, and contexts. He was constantly aware of what it meant to adjust to the ego that was necessary in working with the religious leaders as opposed to what was needed in teaching the disciples. To those with big egos like the Pharisees, he was not afraid to come out strong, calling them a "brood of vipers," suggesting they were offspring of Satan himself (Matthew 12:34). To those with weaker egos, he was not afraid to show vulnerability, weeping at the tomb of Lazarus and crying out to God in front of those who grieved (John 11:35). Yet in all of his contextual sensitivity, Jesus remained true to his ego, balancing it with what it meant to be the Word made flesh among us.

He had every right to be self-centered and arrogant. He was there at the beginning, and all things were created through and for him (Colossians 1:16). He had every reason to be a narcissist, demanding the admiration of others. After all, every creature in the heavens, the earth, and under the earth will one day worship him (Revelation 5:13). But instead, Jesus chose to lower his ego so much that he was born as a baby, subjecting himself to full dependence as a child. He chose to work with his hands, likely learning from Joseph, knowing that life could be created by just a word from his mouth. Jesus submitted himself to the ways of the world, even leading to his own crucifixion, but he did so without losing his sense of identity. In many ways, the great "I Am" surrendered to death precisely because he knew who he was.

His identity was so clear and his ego was so well defined that he did not depend on the affirmation of others. Jesus never had to question whether he was true or relevant or loved because his identity was deeply connected to his relationship with the Father. Jesus was because God is. By trinitarian design, God the Father, God the Son, and God the Spirit exist together, affirming seamless relationship and unique expression all at once. In this way, Jesus knew who he was because the primary marker of his identity came from what John described in the opening of his Gospel: "In the beginning was the Word, and the Word was with God, and the Word was God" (John 1:1). His ego stemmed from this reality and from this very present love. Yes, the ego of Jesus was rooted and grounded in the unconditional, never changing love of God. This love showered Jesus at both his baptism and his transfiguration, speaking from the heavens about the "Son, whom I love" (Matthew 3:17; 17:5). This love anchored Jesus when he was tested by others, strengthening his resolve to stand firm in acts of healing and works of grace (John 5:20). Ultimately, the love of God through Jesus is what punctuates the relevance of the cross, knowing that the crucifixion of the Son was an expression of the Father's deep love for us all (John 3:16). He was willing to die and to surrender his ego for the love of God, which resulted in unimaginable love for us as well.

The death of Christ included the crucifixion of ego as well. For what greater sacrifice can be made on earth than to sacrifice one's sense of self and well-being for the sake of others? The ego fights for self-preservation and justification. It competes with others for its own survival, and without it, we might not consider our lives worth living. But Jesus modeled the duality of deep confidence and true humility by knowing who he was and simultaneously laying it all down. His sense of self was so rooted in his relationship with the Father that he not only loved the world but also encouraged his disciples to be known by this nonsensical love as well (John 13:34-35). The affection Jesus commanded his disciples to have for others did not make sense because it appeared that the world did nothing to merit God's love. In fact, the actions of the world suggested the exact opposite: a hatred of God through Christ and a disdain for those who follow him. But with an ego so strong and a love so deep that it was unafraid of the world, Jesus was still willing to die for it and to call his disciples to a level of self-assurance that enabled them to extend this same kind of love.

EGO, RESURRECTED

For those who are willing, the call to crucify ego comes with the call to know who you are in Christ. It is a call to sacrifice a sense of self that protects and defends for a sense of self that loves and gives. When we willingly submit our egos to be crucified with Christ, what is resurrected is a sense of ego that is deeply rooted in the knowledge and love of God. Paul experienced this profound death and life when he said, "I have been crucified with Christ and I no longer live, but Christ lives in me. The life I now live in the body, I live by faith in the Son of God, who loved me and gave himself for me" (Galatians 2:20). As we know, Paul was no stranger to ego. By his own admission, he was a Pharisee of Pharisees and more obedient to the law than his peers (Acts 23:6, 26:5, Philippians 3:5). He was willing to establish ego-centrism when it was necessary to lead or to be heard, but he was also willing to boast in his weaknesses for God's power to be visible through him. It seems that his duality of strength and weakness came from his relationship with

Jesus in the same way that Jesus' duality came from his identity with the Father. Knowing that he was qualified enough to be called by God and loved enough to be willing to die is what gave Paul the same type of confident humility modeled by Jesus. When Paul sacrificed his ego for the sake of the gospel, what was resurrected was not simply a humbler self-effacement but a more confident identity linked to the love and knowledge of God. This confidence is what allowed him to be "all things to all people," flexing between strength and weakness, boldness and humility, egotism and meekness in various contexts with the singular purpose of glorifying God and building the body of Christ (1 Corinthians 9:22).

What would it look like for you to take a similar approach? While the invitation to crucify the ego applies to all leaders, how this is executed (literally) depends on the factors already articulated, including your context, your worldview, and your personality. While the *how* of crucifixion may vary, the *what* remains the same: for leaders to be more like Christ, what we know of ourselves must die so that what God knows of us can live. For some, crucifying ego may include denouncing some tendencies that keep us too proud: self-reliance, arrogance, superiority, and extreme independence. For others, the process of crucifixion may include surrendering negative habits induced by small egos: insecurity, low self-esteem, extreme self-deprecation, and impostor syndrome. Regardless of what must be torn down in crucifixion, what is revived in resurrection is the simplicity and mystery of the profound love of God.

Being anchored in the all-surpassing love of God is the only thing that will give us strength to moderate our egos for the glory of God and the good of others. And we cannot do this by ourselves. Since we cannot be trusted to self-regulate, God's deep and abiding love can humble us when needed and build us up when we fall short. This love is noted as the motive for discipline, reminding us that God cares enough to correct and rebalance our egos as often as necessary (Hebrews 12:6). The power of God's love is the only foundation that can keep us simultaneously grounded when egos are tempted to expand and lifted when egos are tempted to go low. The love of God is what tempers us with both the overwhelming assurance of our existence and the tremendous modesty of knowing that God does not need us to fulfill his promises. Leaders wrapped in this love, demonstrated through Christ and fueled by the Holy Spirit, can make room to lead and care for others, even as they are led and cared for by God themselves. In short, we cannot lead without love. Knowing God's love for us establishes the ego that is necessary to lead with the confidence of a lion while serving with the unpretentiousness of a lamb.

LEADING LOVED

The ego is complex and nuanced, but once crucified in Christ, it can be the greatest asset of any leader. As we resurrect the ego that is encapsulated by God's love, we also redefine ourselves in a way that is both within and above the world around us. We become new, as Paul suggests, locating our ego and identity in a person and reality that extends beyond the world we know (2 Corinthians 5:17). So again, what would it look like for you to lead with an ego so anchored in God's love that you can be who you are called to be in any given context, at any given moment? Responding to this question requires a lifelong journey in partnership with God's Spirit. As you proceed along this beautiful path, here are some questions that may guide you along the way:

1. What contexts bring out the best of your ego? Which ones bring out the worst?
2. What barriers keep you from truly experiencing the love of God?
3. Where do you feel most compelled to lean into a deeper awareness of God's approval, acceptance, and affirmation?
4. Where do you feel most convicted and encouraged to lean into a deeper knowledge of God's ability to humble you?
5. Describe what it would look like for you to lead like you are deeply loved. What feels different within you? How does this show up differently in your work with others?

May God give us grace to lead like we are deeply loved and to love those we serve from that reality.

5

CRUCIFYING SPEED

*From Deliberately Fast
to Delightfully Slow*

THE PRESSURE OF THE PACE

"Move fast and break things." This was the motto of
Facebook until 2014 and remains the underlying sentiment
of millions of leaders around the world. Considering the
rapid pace of change in the world, this statement attempts
to encapsulate the idea that you must move fast without fear
if you're going to beat the competitors. For some, speed is
everything, especially in leadership. Attentive acceleration
can lead to market advantage. Making good, quick decisions can create stability for the team. The ability to pivot
quickly in times of change can save entire organizations
from going under.

The year 2020 became the perfect example of this fact.
For most leaders at the start of 2020, it was time to put the

planning from the previous year into action. The fiscal year was either just starting or it was hitting its stride at the halfway mark. The outlooks for the year were playing out just as we planned . . . until March of that year when everything changed. Leaders had to make quick decisions about where and how teams should work, where and how products should be sold, where and how services would be provided. There was little time to consider the pros and cons of in-person versus online worship or office-based versus remote working. Leaders had to move quickly to preserve the core or to capitalize on the moment.

Some small business owners found that their production escalated overnight. Home improvement companies had to scale up quickly and even turn away clients as people clambered to upgrade the spaces that turned into quarantine caves. Delivery services had to hire teams quickly as demand nearly tripled, and online fitness programs were bursting at the seams with new subscribers. Simultaneously, some business instantly struggled with loss. Those who were already on the edge were tipped over by pandemic trends. Department stores and those specializing in "workwear" filed for bankruptcy as sweatpants and loungewear took over. Movie theaters and travel companies took significant hits as access was limited and health concerns reigned for more than twenty-four months. Whether scaling up or scaling down, every leader in 2020 was forced to think fast and act quickly to guide organizations through chaos. In many ways, this period of history became a case study in the challenges and opportunities of speed and haste.

Yes, speed and timing are everything in leadership, but it's whose timing that matters most. As the head of a team or organization, it's easy to think the timing at stake is set by you. Leaders determine the pace for others, and organizations cannot outpace the head. This puts gravity on the idea of leaders as the sole source of pace and haste. Add to that societal pressures to always stay on top, always be ahead of the game, and always know what's coming next, and you have a perfect storm of anxious speed. I've heard the same narrative from countless leaders who feel like they and their organizations are on an ever-speeding treadmill race to succeed within their fields. Like hamsters on a wheel, they feel like business or ministry never stops and they keep running faster thinking they'll catch a breath only to find themselves in a faster, panicky pant.

Christian leaders from every sector, no matter how rooted they are in faith, cannot seem to fight the pull to go faster and keep up or to accelerate to beat the crowd. Pastors rush to the finish with sermons crafted every week in hasty anxiety to get it done and sound like the clips they've heard online. Business leaders burn the proverbial candle at both ends, rising before the sun and not sleeping until it's soon to rise again just to catch the first worm and be the first to test a new market. Church planters breathe in the haste of developing communities in untouched spaces, praying and hoping to be the first ones to attract that crowd, build in that neighborhood, or speak that cultural language. Parachurch leaders, all too aware of their noncompetitive fields of Christian competition, ache for bragging rights to be the first to innovate, the first to try, the first to fail and reset and try again, knowing that return on investment (ROI) in ministry still requires being the best. The pressure to go faster and faster can feel like a whirlwind, tossing and turning leaders in different directions each time the societal winds blow. Speed like this is required to know what's coming next, to understand what's relevant, and to keep pace with the trends of attracting new clients, customers, or congregants.

LEADERS ON SPEED

In order to keep this pace organizationally, leaders have to learn to live fast lives. They must discover the secrets of moving quickly and working efficiently to stay ahead of the game. They hurry through their days with each minute allocated and spent like a well-budgeted dollar, not allowing even a penny to be wasted in a mad dash to be the best. With speed, they can be the most efficient, the best equipped, the fastest to finish, and the overall winner.

Speed doesn't just allow us to win, it lets us turn our competitors into losers, which is what really matters to most. Speed means that we can make mistakes, as long as we are the first to finish. We can mess up the words, as long as we say it first. In some cases, we don't even have to be accurate or truthful or have integrity, as long as we're fast and first. This kind of speed has little regard for the people around us because speed like this is within us. It absorbs every fiber of our being, concurrently pulling our bodies, our minds, our emotions, and our souls into a vehicle that moves at 100 miles per hour in a 55-miles-per-hour lane.

Fast-paced leadership is like leading on speed, literally. It affects every part of our bodies, minds, and souls, often making it difficult to slow down, even when it's time to rest on a day off or go to sleep. Leaders who crave speed are always looking for the next best thing and always pushing themselves and their teams to drive forward to an invisible finish line that never exactly arrives. With speed like this, leaders don't have time to deal with employees that appear weak, staff members who move slowly, or teams that under-perform. If they can maximize every moment, then teams should too. If they don't make time for small talk, then no one else should either. When it comes to speed, time spent in idle conversation is like watching money slip down the drain. There is literally no time to talk, no time to meditate, and no time to overthink. When speed is the goal, leaders must live fast to lead fast, and anyone who's not up to speed can get out of the way.

Because the world incentivizes speed, it also accepts the side effects as simply part of leadership. The pace of business requires that leaders live with regular anxiety, constantly concerned about the market, the competitors, the next design, and the next dollar. We accept that leadership means needing something to wake up in the morning and something to help you sleep at night just to keep up with the day. Societal speed means always functioning at peak efficiency, consistently navigating multiple demands at once and still having to come up on top at the end of the latest workday in the organizational time zones. The only way leaders can do this is to pay the price of the fast life by cutting out what the heart needs to get what the hand wants. The heart of the leader needs margin and downtime in order to foster creativity and innovation. But speed requires that leaders sacrifice margin to get more partners, more projects, and more provision in hand. When the heart calls for less, speed forces the hand to demand more of whatever it takes to get to the finish as quickly as possible. This leads to constantly living with FOMO (fear of missing out), fearful of missed opportunities, aware of what the competition is doing, and always ensuring that every resource is maximized and every avenue is exploited to win the race and conquer the goal.

Leaders caught in this relentless race against time are usually exhausted, fearful, and overwhelmed, but they hardly ever confess this way of life because it's become quite easy to conceal. From micro dosing during the day to alcohol binging at night, society has made it easy for leaders to go fast at all times. The market is full of legal (and illegal) ways to keep your hands going when your heart indicates the need to stop. This allows those with the most power and influence to maintain a pace that can be difficult for others on the team to maintain. Most good leaders understand that you can only go at the pace of the team or at the speed of trust within the organization.

But when a leader is living on the thrill of a faster pace, hardly anyone is good enough to keep up. Staff members might find themselves consistently discouraged when their answers don't come fast enough or when projects never measure up to the expected pace of completion. They may come to work and discover that they've been replaced by outside consultants or new hires who can get things going faster. Those best equipped to weigh in on organizational direction may find themselves constantly cut out of major decisions, being told that there's never enough time for proper risk assessment or deliberation for a new idea.

When leaders idolize speed, their personality and preferences often leak into the whole organization, prioritizing what is fast and demoting what feels slow. The preference for speed can affect personnel decisions (hiring and promoting people who get it done quickly over those who get it done right), finances (spending more to get it faster instead of waiting and saving), and ultimately team culture (placing greater value on quantity over quality, completion over precision). While speed leaders may get awards for coming in first place, they often come in last for accuracy, accountability, and sustainability. Sometimes, the consequences of what must be corrected aren't worth the reward of being the fastest in the field.

FAILING FAST

It was 1984 and the executives at the Coca-Cola Company believed they had a problem: their beloved Coke was losing its foothold in the market. Times were changing fast and so were people's desires. They wanted more diet sodas as they watched Jane Fonda and Richard Simmons sweat it out on television screens. When they did drink soda, they wanted it sweeter like the ever-popular competitor, Pepsi. Thanks to the "Pepsi Challenge" of the mid-'70s and its related marketing, everyone knew that Pepsi won taste tests around the nation, and not by a small margin. Bothered by the decrease in sales and the growth of the competition, Coca-Cola executives made a fast decision: mimic the competition with a new product that might save sales. After investing nearly $4 million in the innovation and conducting more than 200,000 blind taste tests, the conclusion was that the new product had a better taste than the competition. With faith in taste alone and fear of losing market share, Coca-Cola introduced "New Coke" on April 23, 1985, as what CEO Roberto Goizueta called, "the surest move ever made."[1] They were convinced that taste was what mattered most, so they didn't take the time to assess any other factors. While some reports indicate that as many as 10 to 12 percent of taste testers were opposed to the new formula and that those with negative views tended to sway the entire focus group, executives may have already decided to advance the innovation, thereby ignoring any dissention.[2]

Goizueta and his team not only moved quickly, they also moved publicly. They invested in public advertising and press releases about the new, tastier Coke, the first formula change in almost one hundred years.[3] They implemented New Coke rapidly, aiming to replace what was already on the market with what was now being mass produced. Unfortunately, negative reactions to this change were even more prompt and public. Within a matter of days, consumers complained about the idea of a new formula, pulling on an emotional attachment to the original Coke they knew and loved. Loyalists felt abandoned and betrayed by the new taste, some feeling that changing the formula was akin to blasphemy. Groups like Old Coke Drinkers of America formed to protest the decision and the Coca-Cola Company received thousands of calls from incensed devotees every single day. With such a significant backlash to the new product and intense pressure from the public, Coca-Cola executives knew that something had to be done. By July 10, 1985, just seventy-nine days after launch, Goizueta and then-president and chief operating officer Donald Keough announced that they were going back to the original. Coke Classic was reintroduced, and within a matter of months, New Coke had silently drifted away. At one point, Keough admitted that while the new taste was clear in research, they miscalculated the "deep and abiding emotional attachment to original Coca-Cola felt by so many people."[4]

Fortunately for the Coca-Cola Company, this rapid marketing failure became one of the most important lessons for their future innovations and new brands. Having learned from the past, the company now creates new brands without replacing what is tried and true. Today, they test beyond taste, gauging other factors like emotional and physical trends in the market along with brand loyalty. It's not that they've stopped moving fast; rather, they've adjusted their pace to better reflect what the market can handle. The company has also used the New Coke lessons to partner more efficiently with adjacent brands, bringing in new product lines, including Sprite, Smartwater, AHA sparkling water, and more.

> We hear a lot about speed to market these days. But speed by itself isn't a competitive advantage—anyone can go fast. The key is identifying potential big bets, starting small and learning before making significant investments and launching at scale. That's what we do.[5]

What most perceived as failure became the key to paced production that starts small and slow in everything and only goes big and fast with a few. The issue with New Coke was not that they went fast. It was that they went fast in a big way that was motivated by fear and set on the competitor's time frame.

WHO OWNS THE CLOCK?

It's worth restating the fact that speed and timing are important in leadership, but it's whose timing that matters most. There are times in life and leadership when we must move quickly and when the pace of the present can make or break the sustainability of the future. But if the pace is only set by the competition, the market, the personality of the leader, the fear of loss, or the thrill of winning, we will lose something (or someone) significant every single time. The only way to lead successfully in our fast-paced world is to let God keep the clock and adjust our sense of timing to his. When God sets the pace, we can go fast or slow, make quick decisions or take our time, knowing that we are exactly where we need to be. This requires that we crucify our sense of speed, often fearful and anxious, to resurrect God's pace that is divine, deliberate, and, usually, delayed. While there are certainly instances in life and Scripture where God moves fast and accelerates his promises, much of the Bible and our journeys with God bear witness of One who moves more slowly and intentionally than we would prefer. God, who is Alpha and Omega and owner of all time, moves with a sense of time and space that is completely different from our own. The One who has shaped eternity and crafted every zeptosecond of the earth's existence has an understanding of timing that goes beyond anything humanity could ever imagine. And while we know that God's timing is perfect as a reflection of God's perfection and sovereignty, Christian leaders might also confess that waiting on God's timing can feel flawed and less than ideal. It is easier to pace yourself by what you see, as situations unfold before you, than it is to pace yourself by what you cannot see. And yet this is exactly what is necessary if we want to lead more like Christ. If we truly want to win by eternal standards, we must learn to live on eternal time, not moved by pressures and impulses that we see on earth, but by God whose ways and times extend beyond our comprehension. And how can we pace ourselves according to a time we cannot fully know or in line with a God whose very existence is beyond what we can grasp? For this, we look to Christ as the image of the invisible and the tangible witness of the intangible God.

IT'S HIS TIME TO TAKE

Lazarus was alive when word came to Jesus that he was sick. He was alive and still had a chance to be healed by his friend. From previous accounts, we know that Jesus didn't have to be present for a person to be cured. The centurion's servant was healed the very moment Jesus spoke the word without even going to his house. Jesus offered to go but then marveled at his faith when he said, "Lord, I do not deserve to have you come under my roof. But just say the word, and my servant will be healed. For I myself am a man under authority, with soldiers under me. I tell this one, 'Go,' and he goes; and that one, 'Come,' and he comes. I say to my servant, 'Do this,' and he does it" (Matthew 8:8-9; Luke 7:7-8). All Jesus did was speak the word and the servant was made whole. The same thing happened to the Syrophoenician woman's daughter who was healed from an evil spirit with just one word from the Lord (Matthew 15:21-28; Mark 7:24-30). The same was true for the Capernaum official's son who was on the verge of death but healed from his affliction as soon as Jesus said he would live (John 4:46-54). With evidence from these past experiences, all Jesus had to do was speak a word and Lazarus, the friend he knew and loved, would have lived. But Jesus did not speak a word to heal from a distance. He did not even make plans to go the moment he heard about the sickness. Instead, he chose to hold off on healing and to delay his travel, waiting two full days before he went to see the one everyone knew he cared about.

The competition would have demanded faster action as spiritualists and mediums of the time advertised rapid results. The market would have insisted on brand consistency, inviting Jesus to be the same for Lazarus as he was for the others he healed, perhaps with VIP treatment and rewards for close friends. The fear of losing more disciples who were waiting to see how Jesus treated those he loved would have driven him to act fast to retain the client base and increase the net promoter score. But he waited.

Unmoved by the competition and unfazed by the possibility of loss, Jesus waited to go see his friend, and while he waited, Lazarus died. By worldly estimations, it appeared that Jesus lost the race against the clock of life, but divine timing suggested that he waited it out. He waited until the clock struck midnight, until the last grain fell in the hourglass, until the final bell rung on the round just to make sure that time was up according to the standards of humanity. While death always signals the end of our time and motivates the race against our proverbial clocks, Jesus demonstrated that this sense of time was not his own. His time was set by God and not by man, allowing him to move at a pace that did not make sense to those who watched. With prophetic impulse and divine dedication, Jesus waited out our clock to demonstrate who really owns the clock and who really tracks the time.

Arriving "late" on the scene gave Jesus the chance to do more than just heal Lazarus. He came to be present so that he could ignite faith in his disciples, comfort the grieving, prophesy of his resurrection, weep over death, declare

God's glory, acknowledge God who hears, raise the long dead, and cause many others to believe. The pace of his timing was not limited to the miracle of healing alone but to everything else that was attached to it as well. In this moment Jesus proved, again, that his time involves more factors and variables than we could conceive and brings fruit that makes the delay worth it in the end. He may have intentionally delayed, but his timing set the pace by a new standard that defied the ways of the world and denied conventional practices. Jesus took his time because it was his time to take. The reality of his lordship made room for impossible results in an unrealistic time frame with unbelievable slowness and remarkable speed.

RESETTING THE CLOCK

Perhaps this is the outcome we long for. Maybe we're longing for this level of miraculous results in impossible time frames, and we think that speed will get us there. If we move fast enough and go hard enough, we just might reach the ridiculous goals we've set for ourselves. But just as New Coke didn't win by getting out there fast and Jesus didn't try to get there first, we won't win with speed or haste if we are not anchored in values that go beyond time. Crucifying speed allows us to relinquish our addiction to the fast-paced life in pursuit of a reset of time altogether. More than speed or slowness, God invites us to reframe the way we think about time; not ours but his, not according to the market but according to eternity, not keeping up with competition but staying in step with the Spirit. The story of Lazarus can become a divine incentive that reminds us to wait on God to get what we really want. Jesus gives us permission to trade in haste for attentiveness and speed for divine deliberation. This does not mean we won't go fast, but it does mean we will go at the pace of God's word and commit to move only when God speaks.

As audacious as this may sound, waiting on God's "go" gives us confidence to lead teams that need to swim against the competitive tides. Spending time with God to authentically hear from him gives us authority to point organizations in a direction that is littered with grace and cluttered with mercy. Like Harriet Tubman, who was known to stop those following her on the underground railroad to literally hear from God, Christian leaders can develop the disciplines to hear both the direction and the pace of God's promises that can lead to the fruit we desperately want to produce. It is true that there are plenty of leaders who believed they were actively listening for God and took a wrong turn. There are many more employees and staff members who have experienced leaders who said they were listening and still went on warp speed, leaving their teams and followers to languish in the dust. But the purpose of crucifying speed is so that God's grace-filled timing may be resurrected. We cannot control every outcome, but we can purposefully set our intentions on God's timing and embrace the grace and mercy that comes in our human attempts to join his pace. As you reset your own sense of time, I invite you to consider these reflections with your team:

- *Make room for collective discernment.* As a key element to minimize harm, making room for trusted individuals to discern the pace together can keep people from feeling left behind. Setting the pace together helps leaders to cultivate trust that will lead to speed at just the right time.

- *Seek impact over impulse.* Beyond the appeal of impact can be a thirst for lasting effect that can overcome the impulses of the day. While acting on an urge can get you there fast, acting with a view toward longer-term impact will help you stay. Impulses tend to fade while impact tends to last.

- *Put the right drivers in the seat.* What people, problems, or pressures are driving the need for speed? We often don't realize that we are being driven by false realities until it's too late. Take the time to assess who or what is driving your pace and make sure that the driver can be trusted to take you in the direction of God's calling.

- *Reclaim the sacramental slow.* With ever-increasing pressures to be fast, leaders will have to be intentional about instituting slower rhythms. This can be as simple as blocking "think days" on the calendar to step off the moving treadmill, building checks and balances into decision-making that take time to ensure that every decision isn't rushed, or even pausing after each meeting or gathering to return space to God and reflect on what is next. Slow can be exercised like a sacrament when it is intentionally engaged in partnership with God.

- *Embrace loss.* Following God's pace might lead to a few missed opportunities, deadlines, or rewards. But God never promised that we would not experience loss, only that our losses would be minimized in light of what we gain with him. We may lose elements in the world, but when we follow his timing, we will gain the eternal value of our souls (Matthew 16:26).

Life is fast and getting faster. Leadership is filled with pressure to speed to the finish and to be the first in the field. But the invitation to forsake the pace of the world in exchange for the pace of God's timing will give us more peace than we could ever imagine in this world. With this nonanxious pace of leadership, God can bring the kind of healing through us that our teams and employees so desperately need.

6

CRUCIFYING PERFORMANCE

From Transactional Performance to
Transformational Presence

ORIGINS OF PERFORMANCE

Do you remember what it felt like to give your first good performance as a child? You can probably remember the sounds of adoration that came after reading the line, the clapping of approval after finishing the song, the pat on the back after running the play, or the cheering of the crowd after scoring the goal. Or perhaps your first performance was celebrated more subtly, like the wink from a teacher when you got the best grade, the fist bump from a friend when you got the right answer, or the internal high-five you gave yourself when you did what others thought you could never do. Our childhoods are often filled with some moment in time when we learned what it felt like to offer a good performance. Whether celebrated privately with a nod of approval or publicly with a proud display, we have all embraced the reality that performance is a key ingredient to success in life.

Conversely, we can also remember the embarrassment of childhood failures, both our own and people we knew. We can remember what it felt like to miss the mark, to disappoint the crowd, or to underperform. We remember how quickly applause can turn to pity or how pity turns to disgrace. All of us remember the student who tripped over the instruments at the band concert, the actor who forgot their lines in the play, the child who had an accident on the stage, or the soloist who stood frozen in front of the microphone for too long. This first glimpse of failed performance becomes etched in our minds as a reminder of the possibility of what can happen when we take the stage.

Whether consciously or subconsciously, we tend to carry these feelings around performance into adulthood and into our ideas of leadership. After all, there are some who believe that leadership is all about performance. We are assessed by the ways that we perform on the job, by our performance with teams, and by the way we lead in comparison to others. Performance-based leadership can be a natural part of leading teams and, in some sectors, may be necessary to help us achieve our goals. But performance in and of itself can take us away from the truth of God's purpose for our lives. It can deceive us into thinking that we must perform to please others or, even worse, to please God. It can cause us to see our work lives as synonymous with our stage lives, accompanied by constant pressure for visible success and the anticipation of rousing applause.

When leadership becomes all about performance, it can awaken within us the extreme behaviors that accompany crowd pleasing and fear of failure. We can find ourselves using performance reviews as competitive assessments, driving our teams to unnecessary lengths to perform well against other teams and organizations, or even using others as examples of the performances we want to avoid. To succeed at job performance is to secure a spot in the next step on the ladder. It suggests that you and your team might gain the recognition and affirmation that makes the work worthwhile. But performance-based success is often short lived, and the end of the applause signals the beginning of the next performance. To fail at this performance is to fail at life and be potentially disqualified from leadership altogether. As stage lights spotlight the main actor, performance-based leadership has the potential to spotlight our pride and amplify our flaws in unhealthy ways.

While this performance-based mindset can be an opportunity for high performers who use failure as fuel, it can be especially harmful for those who have faced trauma associated with performance in the past. For traumatized communities, individuals, and teams, the pressure to perform can be extremely stressful. It can be interpreted as pressure to become someone you are not or to perform for others at the expense of your own health and healing. For some, this pressure can trigger performance anxiety, causing people to panic, freeze, or, on the opposite spectrum, to burn out from the fatigue of overperformance. Anxiety related to performance-based leadership can cause leaders, even those who excel in their fields, to second-guess their contributions, causing them to do twice as much work to prove to themselves and others that they are still worthy of the applause.

The traumas of performance-based leadership are especially harmful when they lead us to believe that we are nothing more than what we do. We can start to see ourselves as being only as good as our last presentation or only as valuable as our last sermon. With this mindset, we tend to evaluate ourselves by what we do alone, constantly trying to outperform our last success or the people we perceive to be high achievers around us. This process of becoming your performance can slowly rob leaders of their identities, turning them into human doings in place of human beings. The real and imagined pressure of being assessed at all times can even cause staff members to separate themselves from their work, competing only for a good review instead of fully embracing the roles they must play. Perhaps this is why Gallup noted that only 14 percent of employees believe that performance reviews inspire them to improve.[1] In an environment where performance is only about missing the mark or pleasing a superior, there is very little motivation to believe that you'll be seen as anything more than what you do.

A PICTURE OF PERFORMANCE-BASED LEADERSHIP

Truth Church was one of the fastest growing churches in America.[2] The young founder started with just a few people

in his home and soon grew to more than one thousand in-
person attendees and five thousand online views in less than
five years. Their vision was to see the entire world redeemed
for Christ, and their mission was to transform every lost soul
into a soul winner for Jesus. As the church grew, the need
for full-time staff also grew. The elders saw the vision and
asked the pastor not to settle for less when it came to
building his team. They raised additional funding to offer
top dollar for each role, recruiting and hiring only the best
to actualize the vision. Over time, the staff at Truth Church
became known to be the very best of the best in their fields,
from ministry to operations. They may have been small in
number, but they were mighty. Most of the staff members
came from secular fields, leaving jobs at banks, tech startups,
and law firms to work at the church. The ministry team was
composed of the country's best teachers, and most had
stunning reputations beyond the church. The AV team
could have worked for any creative marketing agency, and
the sound team was drafted from a leading musical artist.

They were qualified. They were capable. They were
high-capacity performers on weekends, but when Monday
morning came, they all knew what to expect. During
Monday staff meetings, after four services over the
weekend, the dream team was subjected to weekly performance reviews by the executive pastor. They would sit together, review video from each service, pausing on places
where mistakes were made, discuss what went wrong, and
promise to make it right for the next time. Over time, they
learned to compete against each other for the affirmation

of leadership. They would tell their ministry teams, "Well, at least we weren't as bad as the music ministry last week," or "At least we didn't mess up like the welcome team." If anyone was critiqued for making the same mistakes repeatedly, they were ostracized and passively removed from those duties altogether. While turnover was surprisingly low, the performance environment left talented staff members calloused and immune to the worship they so faithfully delivered. The more they performed, the less they felt connected to God, to the church, and to the mission. They were gifted in their jobs, but the performance pressure took away the joy of serving and the value of noncompetitive success.

THE EFFECTS OF PERFORMANCE-BASED LEADERSHIP ON TEAMS

Truth Church is just one example of a community longing for excellence at the expense of genuine thriving. While the senior leader and the general congregation may feel the effects of ministry excellence, the middle management of the church are often the ones who carry the brunt of this cost. The same is true in both profit and nonprofit sectors that are driven by performance. The CEO and customers are often the farthest removed from the challenges that affect staff members and employees driven by high-performance expectations. In each case, team members who have experienced any level of trauma related to performance must choose between isolating themselves from the collective pressure (heads down), striving to be perfect

within the pressure (heads up), or checking out of the
pressure altogether (heads out).

Heads-down performers. One way that staff members and
employees can choose to survive high-performance environments is to simply keep their heads down and do the
work in front of them in hopes of staying out of the extremes of being either too good or too bad. They remove
themselves from opportunities to collaborate with others
for fear that such collaborations would hinder their own
independent success. They turn on when it's time to
perform their roles and turn off when the job is done. It's
likely that these individuals may have endured some level
of performance-based trauma in the past that has taught
them to just lay low and do the job to avoid penalty. While
they may perform well within their lanes, they have little
motivation or desire to do anything other than what they
are paid to do. This type of survival damages the potential
for both individual and collective success, making it nearly
impossible to envision the possibilities of what could
happen if they saw beyond what was directly in front
of them.

Heads-up performers. Staff members and employees who
constantly strive for approval and perfection in high-
performance environments may also be responding in unhealthy ways. Perhaps traumatized by fear of failure in the
past, these individuals are constantly going above and
beyond to be affirmed not simply for doing the job but for
doing it better than anyone else. Their heads look up
toward leadership, ignoring others next to or beneath

them, in order to hit the mark, overachieve the goal, and remain at the top of their game. They are prone to harm others in order to meet their own needs and are limited in what they can envision for their organizations because they can only see what is handed down from the top.

Heads-out performers. Staff members and employees who check out, either emotionally or physically, have chosen to survive in performance-based environments by not participating at all. These are individuals likely so scarred by previous experiences that they protect themselves through emotional removal. Those who choose to stay often remove themselves completely from the work without any concern for the consequences of low or no performance. They "turtle" in threatening situations, turning into their shells and emotionally disappearing from anything that would cause pain, even if it could cost them their jobs. Simultaneously, those who choose to leave often do so with some remorse, wondering if their departure was a secret surrender and a sign that they were not good enough to compete. Like athletes who quit during the competition, heads-out performers who leave often wrestle with what could have been if they had been different, if the standards were different, or if they could have stuck it out in order to survive. They leave because they cannot keep up and often carry with them the stigma of being quitters or losers by those who remain.

In each of these instances, the traumatized individual affects the team and limits overall organizational potential. Whenever someone chooses to be heads down, heads up, or heads out within a purpose-driven team, they negatively impact the success of the whole by ignoring others in an effort to protect themselves.

FROM PERFORMANCE TO PRESENCE

With pressure to perform from traditional avenues of leadership, one antidote could be the gift of presence over performance. As an alternative to performance, presence attempts to maximize team capacity by focusing on who people are as opposed to simply targeting what they can do. Individuals who prioritize being present on the job can be more productive than those who prioritize their performance. Being present at work allows people to bring who they really are to the success of the team leading to more open communication with others, improved collaboration, and a reduction in performance-related anxiety and stress.

Some may mistakenly assume that presence-based leadership removes the need for performance altogether. They may think that prioritizing who you are gives an excuse for poor performance or makes it possible for people to slack off because they are focusing on themselves. Yet, repeated studies prove that presence does not take the place of performance but increases it. When athletes have space to focus on who they are, they are better at what they do. When leaders encourage individuals to practice presence, they encourage high performing teams.

While the benefits are endless, presence-based leadership is not for the faint of heart. Leading with presence requires a foundational belief that organizations are more effective when people can be themselves on the job. It requires faith in the ideas that we are human beings before we become human doings and that highly effective teams can result from highly present individuals. Moreover, leading with presence requires intentionality within the mind of the leader in order to release that capacity within others. Noted executive coach Kristi Hedges describes it this way: "I define having an intentional presence as understanding how you want to be perceived and subsequently communicating in a manner so that you will be perceived the way you want."[3]

At first glance, it may seem like presence-based leadership is just another way to manipulate people into high performance. However, what Hedges notes is the precise reason why more leaders lean on performance as opposed to presence: because you cannot bring out of others what you do not already have within yourself.

Presence-based leadership demands present leaders. In an age where everything and everyone claims our attention at all times, presence requires an intentional silencing of external noises in an effort to be fully available to what is before us, one moment at a time. Leadership of presence requires discipline, but if we can harness this gift, it has the capacity to release greater freedom and effectiveness than performance-based leadership could ever provide.

A PICTURE OF PRESENCE-BASED LEADERSHIP

High Hopes was one of the top-rated homeless shelters within its region. They exceeded national turnover rates, moving individuals from homeless to housed in record time. They had a wait list for churches who wanted to partner and were known for receiving grants that enhanced their already stellar services. These grants made it possible for them to deploy the right software and customer relationship management systems to track milestones and demonstrate quantitative impact to stakeholders on a consistent basis. It also gave them ample funding to hire talented staff from across the country to serve in every role. The executive director was always outward-facing, inspiring volunteers and donors to support their ministry and find joy in serving others in the community.

Because of their track records, High Hopes was frequently asked about their secret to success. Some speculated that their high impact was a result of their location in a small city with little homelessness to start. Others suggested that their connections to donors and funding made it impossible for them to fail. Yet, when staff members were asked about the factors that made the organization so successful, they all said the same thing: we just try to be present with people where they are. This presence started with the executive director, who reported having thirty minutes of quiet reflection each day before meeting with the staff. Staff members, some of whom were once clients themselves, shared that they felt seen and heard whenever their leader was with them: "His phone would be ringing, his text messages would be going off, his notifications would ding, and the whole time, he'd be paying attention to each of us."

The leadership he modeled for staff was what he encouraged them to give to those in need. In repeated conversations with churches and partners, he would advise that the best thing anyone could do for a person begging on the street was to ask for his or her name: "When you ask someone for their name and give them yours, you remind them that who they are is more important than what you can do for them or what they can do for you. It changes the conversation from a transaction to a relationship."

THE EFFECTS OF PRESENCE-BASED LEADERSHIP

The High Hopes story is relevant for those who want to serve traumatized employees, staff, and constituents. While not everyone is without a home, it is clear that everyone longs to be seen and valued for who they are. This example transcends the social services sector, reminding us that leaders with personal presence can be a prophetic presence for others in a way that passes that presence to become part of the organizational DNA.

Personal presence. Presence-based leadership requires leaders who are present to God and to themselves before they attempt to be present to others. While the busyness of the day may cause high-powered leaders to skip moments of meditation and stillness, leaders who take time as little as ten minutes a day to reflect on who they are called to be are far better equipped to help others do the same. Executive coach Luis Costa suggests that fully present leaders must learn to be present to their four selves: the intellectual self, the emotional self, the spiritual self, and the physical self.[4] Being a present leader requires that you take time to tune into where you are intellectually (What is on my mind right now?), emotionally (How am I feeling right now?), spiritually (Where do I see God right now?), and physically (What does my body need right now?). Starting with the spiritual self, leaders who are present with God can be fully vulnerable, bringing to God every part of themselves in order to experience God's presence in every part of their intellectual, emotional, and physical lives. This level of deep presence and vulnerability with God and with self keeps leaders grounded in affirmation that is real instead of performing for an imaginary audience.

Prophetic presence. Leaders who are present to God and to themselves can provide a prophetic presence for others. This type of presence-based leadership doesn't just encourage people to be who they are today, it sees the good that could come from who they could be tomorrow. While performance puts pressure on people to do something they may not be currently doing, presence encourages people to become someone they have the potential to be. For traumatized employees and staff members, presence-based leadership becomes prophetic when leaders can see beyond the pain and even the mistakes of teams to see a story of something far more significant ahead. It takes advantage of the shortfalls, not as failures that define us but as opportunities that reshape us into better people for the future. The prophetic power of presence enables leaders to see both what is and what is to come with an invitation to lean into that vision together.

Passed presence. When leaders practice personal presence for themselves and operate in prophetic presence with their teams, the result is a "passed presence" that begins to permeate the entire organization. Teams that make room for members to be themselves embrace a level of failure and learning that helps them to grow. That growth inspires innovation that can ultimately lead to a transformation, both of the people on the team and of what they can produce together. This ripple effect of growth is what gives presence-based leaders and teams the edge over those focused solely on performance. When the priority is on the people, teams thrive in shared presence with each other. However, when the priority is on performance, the only thing to be passed on to others are the goals and objectives that must be achieved. Performance pressure can stifle the innovation that is possible when presence is embraced. When people know who they are, they can do things they did not know they were capable of doing. Yet when people think they know what to do, they can too easily lose sight of who they are, resulting in a lose-lose situation for themselves and for the organizations they serve.

JESUS: THE PRESENCE-BASED LEADER

Throughout Scripture, we see Jesus as the one who is fully present at any given time and thus able to offer that presence to others. This is especially apparent in Mark 5:1-20 where Jesus healed the demoniac. In this important exchange, Jesus modeled what it means to have personal presence that becomes prophetic presence that inspires a passed presence that changes large groups of people.

Before the stories even begin, the end of Mark 4 reminds us that Jesus was first sleeping on a boat (Mark 4:38). Before he showed up to the urgency of those who needed him, Jesus took the time for personal presence by resting. Rest has a way of helping us to tend to our physical, intellectual, spiritual, and emotional selves at the same time. It is arguably because of this moment of rest, interrupted as it was by the desperation of the disciples, that Jesus was prepared to be present for the man who met him on the shore.

This personal presence of Jesus translated into prophetic presence for the man who lived in the tombs. Immediately upon seeing him for who he was, Jesus commanded the evil spirits to leave him (Mark 5:8). He did not treat this man as others did in the town where he lived, only seeing him for what he did to himself and only knowing him by the way he performed. Jesus saw him first as a traumatized man who needed to be known and delivered. "What is your name?" Jesus asked, speaking both to the man and to the spirits within him (Mark 5:9). With one simple question, Jesus led with prophetic presence, seeing both who the man was in that moment and who he could be. This question changed the scene from a transaction (What do you want with me? [Mark 5:7]) to a transformation (Who are you; what is your name? [Mark 5:9]). With deeply prophetic presence, Jesus' question forced the spirits to identify themselves, which led to their demise and to the man's deliverance. The man who was once present to no one became fully present because of one who saw him in a way that no one else could.

Having experienced the personal and prophetic presence of Christ, the man once known by his possession was now "sitting there, dressed and in his right mind" (Mark 5:15). The result of his deliverance was evident to all by his presence. While he would have preferred to simply stay with Jesus, he was sent by the Lord into his own town and to his own people to show and tell them what happened. When he did, the people were amazed, presumably not just because of what Jesus had done but also because of the presence this once-delusional man now embodied (Mark 5:20). His transformation allowed him to model passed presence that encouraged others to seek the one whose presence changed his life.

EXCHANGING PERFORMANCE FOR PRESENCE

Every day that we lead, we have an opportunity to better serve traumatized teams and constituents by choosing presence over performance. We can choose to stave off the urgency and demands of the day by starting with intentional presence with God for ourselves. We can choose to see people for who they are and who they can be as opposed to judging or even using them for what they can do. We can choose to create institutions and organizations that pass on the gift of presence as a core value of who we are and as a reflection of what we do. As we crucify the amorphous standards for performance, we can experience the resurrection of life, affirmation, and purpose that comes only from our presence in God.

1. What is your earliest memory of performance as a child? What was the reaction of those for whom you performed?

2. How did your childhood experience with performance shape your understanding of performing as an adult?

3. Where do you experience the most pressure to perform in your life today?

4. What would it look like to exchange performance for presence in your personal or professional life?

5. How does the story of Jesus healing the demoniac resonate with you?

6. In what ways could the presence of God change how you see your own presence with others?

7. Write down one small step you could take this week to prioritize presence over performance. Pray and invite God to help you take that step.

7

CRUCIFYING PERFECTION

From Unattainable Standards to Grace-Filled Wholeness

MANE PERFECTION

I was thirteen years old the day perfection wooed me. In hindsight, it probably called to me years before, but I was only able to greet it on this particular day. It was a clear, windy, spring Sunday morning at my grandmother's house in Pittsburgh, and we were going to be late for church. Morning Star Baptist Church was only a block away from the house, so all we had to do was walk right down the hill and we'd be at the front doors. The hurried hustle in the house could be seen, felt, heard. My sister was getting ready in the bathroom in Grandma's room, my uncles and aunts were in the guest bathroom and bedroom, and I was getting ready in the hallway because that was the only unoccupied mirror at the time.

My mom and grandmother were calling us from downstairs because we had to be on time; we were "volun-told"
to lead praise and worship at the start of the service. My
aunts ran down the stairs in a flurry of high-heeled shoes in
hands, coats over shoulders, and belt flying in midair, half
on and half off. My sister nearly tumbled down the stairs,
chiding me as she went, reminding me of the fire that was
waiting to consume me from the mouths of my mother and
grandmother if I didn't hurry down the stairs behind her. I
should have gone downstairs. I should have followed the
examples of those who went before me and listened to the
advice from my younger sister. But I could not go down; not
yet. Not until my bangs were perfect.

You see, this was the 1980s when "mall bangs" were done
just right by girls and women of all races and ethnicities.
From Kim Fields of the popular TV show *The Facts of Life* to
Vanna White on *Wheel of Fortune* to Whitney Houston
herself, everyone who was anyone wore mall bangs. You had
to have the right amount of height on the top layer bang,
often swooped over like a tidal wave to the side, held just
right by a light haze of Aqua Net hair spray. You needed the
right amount of bounce, wisp, and curl on the lower bang,
divided in an equal amount to the quantity of hairs in the
top layer bang, also held by said holding spray. Everything:
every hair, every part, every wisp had to be just right, and I
stood there, in the hallway mirror at Grandma's house,
making sure it was exactly as it should be. I stood there long
after I heard the front door open and close with each
person leaving. I stood there after the final warning call

from my sister rang out to me in desperation and fear. I stood there, making sure my mall bangs looked just like *Teen* magazine . . . until I heard my mother's footsteps behind me.

I could see her image rising in my mirror with fabled plumes of smoke emerging from her nostrils and mythical fire on her tongue. I could almost hear the shrill sound of a teapot somewhere in the distance as she got closer and closer, approaching me with a palpable fury. With each step up the stairs, she demanded to know what I was doing, why I was still here, what was wrong with me, and had I lost my mind, all in one breath. I explained to my mother that I needed my bangs to be perfect for church. Those were the exact words that tumbled so carelessly from my mind to my mouth before I could catch them. I was late and still standing in the mirror while everyone else had left the house because I wanted my bangs to be perfect.

Well, let's just conclude by saying that the lesson I learned that day was that there is no such thing as perfect mall bangs when it comes to being on time for church. Also, there is wind. Barely recovered from my mother's scolding, half stumbling with tear-filled eyes down the stairs, I walked outside and remembered the wind. As it blew away my perfect mall bangs, with little concern for the copious amounts of hair spray, I learned that there is no such thing as perfect bangs because there is no such thing as perfect.

THE SEDUCTION OF PERFECTION

As popular as they were, maybe your first taste of perfection didn't come from visions of having the perfect bangs or hair like mine did. Perhaps your first encounter came from realizing a perfect score in a video game or getting a perfect grade on a school assignment. Was perfection revealed when you understood its reward or was it before then, when you discovered that it was possible?

Like Goldilocks, we often meander through our childhood experiences, never quite satisfied with things that are too hot or too cold, only to discover a category in life called "perfect." When the conditions are just right or the game is played just right or the outcome is achieved just right, we begin our tantalizing journey toward the illusion of perfection. Early in life, we understand perfection as a destination. We think, *When I achieve this, I will have reached perfection,* or *When I get to this point, I will arrive at perfection.* But along the way, we realize that perfection is more than just an end, it is also a means. It is more than just a place to arrive, it is also a way of being along the way. You have to be perfect to get to perfection.

In video games, for example, it takes a certain number of correct moves to end a level with a perfect score. In school, we have to get 100 percents on a series of tests and get As in a series of classes before we end with a perfect GPA. And once we reach perfection once, we long for it over and over again. Once we sample the sound of perfect, we long to hear it and experience it with such passion that it can slowly become an obsession. We don't just want the same area to be perfect, but we want perfection in every area. The perfect score on the test creates a yearning for the perfect score at the game, prompting a desire for the perfect relationship, the perfect job, the perfect board, the perfect children, and yes, even enticing us toward perfect hair. What can start as a desired outcome of general excellence can slowly morph into an obsession for perfection that is so personal that we are the only ones who can achieve it.

Like most trappings of the soul, this craving for perfection can come to us in many forms and at many stages, provoked from the outside or developed from within. For some, the external vision for perfection comes to us in childhood, perhaps stemming from a desire to please high achieving parents or guardians. It can be difficult to grow up in a household where the pressure to be perfect comes from parents who seem acutely aware of your inadequacies. Some call this "other-oriented perfection" where the person sees themselves as flawless but others—children, coworkers, partners—are severely deficient and in need of help.[1] Children growing up in these situations may be scrutinized for getting a 98 percent instead of 100 percent on a test. They may win prizes in music but still be forced to practice an instrument until every note is just right or perform above grade level and still be pushed to know and do more than everyone else. The fear of falling short of the high, unattainable standards of a critical parent or caregiver can cause children to believe that perfection is the only way to be seen and heard. They can begin to interpret perfection as love, seeing the achievement of a high standard or goal as synonymous with approval and affection.

Other-oriented perfection is also closely connected to depression in children who are never sufficient and in the adults who are never satisfied.[2] While the idea of reaching "nirvana" spurs them forward, the fact that it never arrives drives them back. History suggests this may have been the case for Wolfgang Amadeus Mozart, who became one of the most well-known composers of Western classical music. He was a child prodigy who began playing at three years old, composing at four, and playing in courts before he turned six. But some say it was his father, Leopold Mozart, who set Wolfgang's eyes toward perfection. He was his child's teacher, manager, and booking agent, continually pushing him to travel and perform and play around the world, at times against his will. Some say it was this drive toward greater levels of exposure that both accelerated and hindered father and son, leading to significant illnesses for most of their lives.[3]

In other cases, perfection can surface from within as a response to trauma or an effort to try to control things when everything else feels out of control. Unlike other-oriented perfection, self-oriented perfection starts internally, either as a reaction or as a personality trait. For example, some children may be inclined toward perfection due to the perception of failure in parents, guardians, or even siblings. In this reaction, they are driven by a desire to be nothing like what they have seen or experienced. This is more than just a decision to stay away from drugs when others have overdosed or to stay away from alcohol in a family of alcoholics. It is a preoccupation with being the absolute best as a counter-reality to what they perceive as the absolute worst.

Similarly, this kind of perfection could be a response to traumatic situations that cause intense fear or anxiety. A focused obsession on excelling in a particular area can be an attempt to counter the internal voices of fear and shame. It can feel like a safe strategy to soothe external pain with a sense of internal excellence. Perfection can capture us with the idea that we are insufficient, inadequate, or inferior in ways that cause us to counter with another narrative of superiority. For example, someone who struggles with how they look may try to be a perfect student to compensate for this area of perceived weakness. Another person who feels like they are lacking in "book smarts" may aim for perfection in personality and charisma to fill the gap.

In each case, perfection comes to them as a coping mechanism that helps them make it through some difficulty with the appearance of ease. And still in other cases, perfection can just be built in the fabric of who we are, wooing us by its power from a very young age. Renowned tennis player Serena Williams reflected on this natural inclination toward perfection, stating,

> I remember learning to write my alphabet for kindergarten and not doing it perfectly and crying all night. I was so angry about it. I'd erase and rewrite that A over and over, and my mother let me stay up all night

while my sisters were in bed. That's always been me. I want to be great. I want to be perfect. I know perfect doesn't exist, but whatever my perfect was, I never wanted to stop until I got it right.[4]

Still others are lured into the grip of unattainable perfection by the society around them. This socially prescribed ideal of perfection taunts young girls into eating disorders and young men into steroids with images of the perfect body. It seduces us into using filters, fixes, and avatars to display the best versions of ourselves to the public. As an increasing reality for each generation, the pressure to reach society's version of perfection affects the rate of social comparison, self-assessment, and social expectations. We have become experts at comparing ourselves to someone better, pros at finding our own deficiencies, and specialists at demanding that people and systems around us all exceed our expectations. While other-oriented and self-oriented perfectionism are on the rise, researchers found that socially prescribed perfection has increased at twice the rate of the other two.[5] This means that the pressure is on to reach societal goals of perfection, and younger generations are most susceptible.

Perfection is defined by every community, often in very different ways, and even those who reach these often-unreasonable standards do so at great cost. They may be perfect in athletics, but it costs them friendships. To be perfect in wealth and career success often costs the health of the family and the well-being of the soul. Regardless of how we are lured into the grip of the unattainable, the obsession of this pursuit may prove to be too exorbitant for the soul.

PERFECT CASUALTIES

When a leader becomes consumed with the idea of what is perfect, it can cause a ripple effect of harm to themselves, their loved ones, and especially to staff and employees. This is because perfectionism cannot be contained. Like that burned popcorn smell that seeps from the microwave, polluting the air and everyone around it for hours after it's been thrown in the trash, a leader's preoccupation with flawlessness oozes into the fabric of the organization and lingers long after the leader is gone. One person's relentless pursuit of perfection can set unreasonable standards for others, creating a near hostile work environment for the team. Everything must always be exact, not just according to the employee's standard but according to leadership.

Furthermore, what the leader believes to be perfect may not even be known to anyone until what is submitted is rejected, often with great disdain or even violent repulsion. This is how some described the deep perfectionism of Steve Jobs, genius and late CEO of Apple.

[Perfection] pushed him to both hurt himself and others. Others have pointed to Jobs's terse behavior with his employees. Some recalled him as "rude, dismissive, hostile, spiteful," writes Gawker's Ryan Tate, who discusses the manipulation Jobs used to "inspire" his workers. Yet, Jobs went beyond the pushy boss, who blows off the handle. "He screams at subordinates," writes Gladwell and once told his public-relations assistant that her suit is "disgusting." He couldn't handle anything less than perfection, and often took it out on others.[6]

The double-edged sword of perfection caused both great success for the company and great harm for Jobs and those around him. At times, this maddening pursuit led to superior products developed in record time. On the other hand, his fixation with perfection created a lag in decision-making, causing him to take weeks on mundane decisions like choosing a sofa or washing machine.[7]

This is more than just a desire to be our best selves or to expect others to do well. Perfectionism is an absolute fixation on a vision of perfect and an unwillingness to rest or settle until that vision is realized. The obsession with an extreme version of excellence is so subversive, so cunning that leaders may not even recognize its possession until it's too late. They may not consider their passion to be harmful until staff members leave or complain, close friends or family intervene, or they are consumed with the personal costs of depression, anxiety, burnout, or worse. Perfectionism in the workplace is often an attraction to those who like challenges, enjoy responsibilities, and frankly, those who like to win. These team members often subject themselves to torturous expectations leading to long days, late nights, and constant mental contortions just to please the exacting boss. While it can be argued that perfection draws perfectionists, calling their allegiance to the organization at the expense of other loyalties and commitments, there is no guarantee that these temperaments and pursuits will lead to any version of success. In these rigorous environments, team members suffer the collateral damage of anguish when decisions cannot be made or stress when actions must be taken to appease.

Perfectionism keeps leaders and teams in constant cycles of paralysis or frenzy, always plagued by the need to grasp an ideal that is consistently beyond reach. Both the leader and those who follow suffer the effects of poor mental health as the angst of decision-making often leads to anxiety and depression. Even when they can see the damaging effects of perfectionism, some leaders cannot let go of their meticulousness and conscientiousness for fear of missing the mark or losing the competitive edge.[8] They are afraid of messing up and worry that lessening of the pressure will lead to poor performance or a lazy embrace of mediocrity. As a result, these leaders may see their perfection as an organizational asset instead of a liability. They may see those who push against their standards as necessary losses instead of casualties, believing that the pursuit is well worth the loss. But what happens when the pursuit of the absolute divides and devours absolutely?

IN PROXIMITY WITH PERFECTION

Perfectionism is a jealous, empty consumption. It leaves no room for anything other than a mirage conjured in our minds that will never truly be attained. It drives us to seek after it, to live for it, and to love it more than anything else. We pant for perfection, like dehydrated survivors in the desert, thirsting for its refreshing waters only to find ourselves lapping at the rough sands of reality. It pushes us to want it above everyone else and to sacrifice anything and anyone to receive it.

Because of the strength of its pull, the only way to correct perfectionism is to crucify it. We must nail to the cross that which seeks to engulf us. For some already held by the grip of the flawless, the fear of killing what we think makes us better can be overwhelming. You may be thinking, *If I let go of this image of what is perfect, even if it doesn't exist, won't I succumb to imperfection? Won't I give in to what is subpar? If I stop striving for what is perfect, won't I cease to exist?* This fear of falling into substandard living and leadership is a valid concern for those truly looking for another way. But to those of us who struggle to release the exactness of what holds us, God says, "have no fear." The same one who calls us to nail perfection to the cross is the only one who is truly perfect. In Christ, we find the only true and loving image of perfection, and we can never reach what our hearts desire without him.

Jesus, fully God and fully man, is the only one who lived sinless among us. He set the standard for those who would follow so that we might be more like him. And just in case we were unsure of what perfection looked like, he gave some specific examples in Matthew 5. In a conversation with crowds and disciples, Jesus laid out what it meant to be perfect. It looks like being blessed in persecution and suffering for faith (vv. 3-12), being salt and light in a bland and dark world (vv. 13-16), fulfilling the righteousness of the law (vv. 17-20), refraining from anger and holding nothing against anyone (vv. 21-26), thinking no lustful thoughts (vv. 27-30), rejecting divorce and remarriage (vv. 31-32), making no oaths and keeping your word (vv. 33-37), not resisting evil (vv. 38-42), and loving your enemies (vv. 43-47). He closed these human impossibilities with one last command: "Be perfect, therefore, as your heavenly Father is perfect" (Matthew 5:48).

But Jesus knew that none of us could ever reach this standard in totality. None of us could be and do all that he spelled out in this chapter, and certainly none of us could be perfect as God is perfect in and of ourselves. But what if Jesus wasn't calling us to do something to be perfect? What if this text was not about doing but about being in relationship with perfection himself? Could it be that our proximity to Christ's perfection would imbue within us rays of divine grace that would be sufficient for our weaknesses? In other words, it could be that Jesus was saying, "Come and be in deep relationship with me and I will give you grace that perfects your imperfections."

Coming up with a list of rules to follow that would lead to perfection is the easy way out. The young man who tested Jesus with his own exactness learned this lesson too well. Matthew shared this story a few chapters later in a perfectionist's encounter with the Perfect One. After sharing that he had followed all the rules, crossed every religious *T* and dotted every *I*, Jesus told the man one last thing he needed to do to reach what consumed him: "If you want to be perfect, go, sell your possessions and give to the poor, and you will have treasure in heaven. Then come, follow me" (Matthew 19:21). The young perfectionist, wanting to be justified in all he had already done, was completely caught off guard by this last requirement. He was so thrown off by what he possessed on earth that he missed the opportunity to be possessed by the eternal. Jesus offered an invitation for this man to become a disciple and to come into proximity with perfection that bestows grace with power to perfect every one of his imperfections. He had a chance to be in relationship with the flawless one who had capacity to make him flawless by association and by his blood, but he missed it. He was so besought by his view of perfection that he missed the chance at earthly excellence that would lead to eternal perfection with Christ. As a result, Matthew says, the man went away sad because he had great wealth.

We often think the man's sorrow is because he had so much to give away. But there's a chance that his deepest sorrow came from the fact that he followed all the rules, met all the requirements of society, climbed all the requisite ladders, and amassed the wealth that others longed for only to be asked to give it away. Perhaps his wealth represented his achievements. Maybe it reminded him that he was the one who did it right, the greatest of his time. We can imagine that this command from Christ is about the same as asking Steve Jobs to give up Apple at the height of his career or asking Serena Williams to give up everything that made her the greatest tennis player of all time just to follow Jesus. The Savior didn't ask whether his pursuit of eternal life came from others, from himself, or from society. He didn't inquire about the pressures he was under or commend the nobility of his request. He simply invited him to give it all away and become a follower of Jesus.

The problem for meticulous people is that we don't reach perfection for anyone else's sakes but our own. For this young man, not even Jesus could take that away. But imagine if he were willing. Imagine if, in that moment, it hit him that all his striving and grasping for perfection meant nothing. What if the chains of the idolatry of perfection were broken and he began to see himself for who he was and Jesus for who he is? Perhaps perfection would be crucified and perfect union with Christ could be resurrected. When we strive toward perfect union with Christ who is in perfect union with God, then and only then can we get a glimpse of the proximity of perfection.

Contrary to the fears of perfectionists, the invitation to crucify perfection is an invitation to be in total and complete union with Christ by the power of the Holy Spirit. The fruit of this dependent union forged through the Spirit is excellence in faith, which might even materialize as excellence by the standards of the world. The operative word here is *might*. Living to be in perfect union with Christ means taking up your cross and following him wherever he leads, even if his leading does not always take you to the top. Sometimes, we are called to follow Jesus into areas that look like failure to the world. Crucifying perfection might lead to less money, loss of power, rejection, or even the death of your career. But what we know about Jesus is that crucifixion is always a precursor to resurrection. When the perfection of our pursuits is crucified, the perfection of our union with him, leading to excellence in the faith, can be resurrected. No, you will never be perfect in and of yourself. But by faith in God through the power of the Holy Spirit, you can live toward perfect union with God until we are perfected in his eternal presence after death. This is God's perfect will.

PRACTICING PERFECT UNION

The act of crucifying other-oriented, self-oriented, and social perfection requires daily devotion. For in the same way that we allowed ourselves to be consumed by perfectionistic ideals, we must now become consumed by sacrificing them before the Savior. When we lay down what we once longed for, we allow God to resurrect within us a longing for the type of relationship with him for which Jesus prayed. Repeatedly in John 17, Jesus prayed that we would be one with him as he was one with the Father. This oneness represents perfect, seamless union, which no human being can achieve alone. In this regard, we must look to God to give us strength to be close to him when the world and everyone else calls us away. We can become excellent in our careers, flawless in our educational pursuits, immaculate in our money management, but none of that matters if we are not moving toward perfect union with God.

As we process this transition from earthly perfection to divine union, here are four questions that may help along the way:

1. *What are you most afraid of?* Fear, like perfection, often paralyzes us, making us feel like we can't possibly let ourselves go. But when we face what we fear, God gives us strength to name the obstacle that he will overcome through us. Name what you are afraid might happen when you crucify your sense of perfection and allow God to deal with it head-on (1 Peter 5:7).

2. *What does it look like to confess your imperfection?* Confession of where we are is the beginning of any transformation. When we confess to God that we are far from perfect, we acknowledge the truth and begin to break down perfection's façade. In the confession of sin and imperfection, we make room for deep dependance on God's forgiveness and grace (1 John 1:9).

3. *Who can you invite on this journey?* Perfectionism is typically enabled by others around us. Whether in our homes or in the workplace, whether family or friends, every perfectionist has someone who fuels us. In order to pivot from who we were to who we want to be, we will need companionship to support us and to flag for us the moments when we regress. Think of people who genuinely care for your well-being and invite them to help you focus less on earthly perfection and more on perfect dependance on God (Proverbs 12:26).

4. *How can you take the first step?* As a recovering perfectionist, you may be tempted to change everything at once . . . or to do nothing at all. It is easy to be overwhelmed by what God desires, but all you need to do now is take the first step. This first step could be taking a deep breath to reset before reacting to people who are less than perfect. It could be pausing a few times a day to pray and ask the Holy Spirit to keep you in union with God. Whatever your step may be, commit to taking it one day at a time with an abundance of grace (Colossians 3:23).

Perfection is not about results but about redemption. No matter how perfect you think you've been or how defective, God can use every part of your life for his glory. The greatest gift you can ever receive is the gift of knowing you are loved by God, not because of what you've done but simply for who you are. God loves you, flaws and all, and the invitation to crucify perfection is the invitation to become immersed in God's unfailing love. As you live into God's love, you will lean toward perfect union with him until Christ comes to make us truly perfect with him.

8

CRUCIFYING LOYALTY

From Collective Assimilation to
Communal Affirmation

THE PRICE OF LOYALTY

Every leader wants a loyal team. We want people who are willing to stick with us through difficulties and remain close during organizational challenges. In the ideal world, we would hire team members who are willing to stay the course and grow with us for as long as we lead. With longevity comes institutional knowledge, and such insights are not easily replaced. Loyal employees are easier to keep and also easier to trust. You don't have to worry about them trading industry secrets or misrepresenting the brand or going to work for competitors. Since they're loyal, they are more likely to stay, which can be one less thing for leaders to worry about.

However desirable it is to recruit and maintain loyal teams, it is also quite dangerous. Loyal team members are least likely to disagree, and even if they do, they tend to keep things moving along. Their dedication to the mission or to the leader can cause them to say yes more often than no and to view agreement as more meaningful than dissent, both for themselves and for others around them. This is especially true in Christian contexts when loyalty to the organization's mission often equates to loyalty to God. In these spaces, it's difficult to distinguish a person's faith in God from their faith in a person or organization. They dedicate themselves to their work as if work was God, tirelessly giving of themselves with a sense of higher purpose and calling. While this may seem like a leader's dream on the surface, what's beneath it can turn into a nightmare of idolatry that gradually draws both leaders and their loyal followers farther away from God.

To love and to cherish: the pastor. The congregation hung on every word he spoke. Ushers and greeters stood silently, without even a cough. The praise team waited in the wings, fanning as quietly as they could to make sure they didn't miss anything. Babies, somehow, simultaneously, stopped crying. The air was still thick with the residue of musical encores, the lights were steadfast in the illumination of the newly built backdrop, bringing the most delicate contrast between an oversized image of the Sea of Galilee and the brilliant white of the pastor's carefully selected robe. Over the gentle murmur of the state-of-the-art HEPA air purifiers, the pastor of the Light Worship Center announced that the church would be starting a new capital campaign to fund a stellar outreach center on the adjacent land.[1]

As founder of this illustrious worship enterprise, he had not stopped working from the moment his family began the church at his humble dining room table. With only eleven people to start, including seven extended family members, the pastor grew the congregation to more than two hundred regular attendees each Sunday. The ones who started as mentees were now lay leaders and associate ministers. The ones who began as early supporters now served as elders, deacons, and board members. Over the years, the pastor had not only built a congregation, he had also formulated a loyal tribe. They had been around long enough to know the pastor and his family inside and out. They blushed in the presence of his rare moments of praise and bristled under his anticipated and regular outbursts of disappointment. Outsiders called him abusive, but inside, they all knew that every anointed man of God had a dark side— one they were selected and chosen by God to protect.

On this particular Sunday, the inner circle studied the congregation from their reserved seats at the front of the sanctuary and at the ends of exclusive rows, watching to assess the loyalty of the members by their reactions to the announcement. The leadership team would be asked to share their observations in the back and would be held accountable for the measure of their disgust with those who did not demonstrate the applause deserving of their spiritual father. They whispered to each other the names of suspect leaders who dared to remain seated rather than stand when the announcement was made and texted the names of wealthy families who were absent from the scene.

While the pastor shared very little strategy around when, how, or why the outreach center would be built, the congregation, and especially those who served in ministry, were expected to be consistent, nay, even more diligent in their financial support. They were expected to applaud him, even when things didn't make sense. They were expected to give, even when the vision was not clear. Most important, the congregation and the staff members were expected to obey the pastor and be faithful to the church, "as unto the Lord," regardless of where the vision took them because everyone in the inner circle knew that the only way to honor the pastor was with faithful loyalty and consistent affirmation.

To love and to cherish: the CEO. The staff still felt a little uneasy being in one room together. They had returned to in-person meetings for a few years now, but it still felt strange sitting so closely to one another. With this proximity, they could feel the nervous energy in the room as chairs scraped quietly while people tried to get comfortable and hear the muffled anxiety of shoes scuffling on the floor as people shuffled closer and stifled sniffles to ensure the voices were heard. The CEO had called an unanticipated all-staff meeting, and everyone knew that could only mean bad news. There were whispers of layoffs and rumors of a staff reorganization. Some speculated that the CEO was planning to leave, while others were sure it had to do with the board.

Once everyone had arrived (because the CEO never started without everyone present and silent), she began with the news that the organization would be going in a new direction. Instead of simply focusing on providing meals for children, they would also be giving away bicycles, thanks to a new partnership with a controversial general merchandise chain. While the decision was risky, she said that it was also necessary to ensure the organization's financial sustainability and fulfill a more expansive mission. As soon as she concluded, the chairman of the board encouraged applause for this innovative decision and asked for the full support of the staff, which would be demonstrated by their unquestioning compliance to what they would be asked to do in this new season. He then handed the microphone to the chief of staff who garnered more applause for the CEO in her thoughtful decisions and asked staff members to work closely with their managers and submit to any new requests. The supervisors and managers were then asked to stand as they, one by one, thanked the CEO for a job well done and confirmed the unquestioning support of her decisions. The last person to take the mic was the director of human resources, who explained that new roles would be added and redundancies would be removed.

The meeting concluded with a standing ovation, led by the board chair and followed by all the organization's executives. They made sure to follow the directions they were given in the pre-meeting just an hour before, when the CEO shared a preview of the announcement with them. Most of the leaders in that meeting disagreed with the decision and tried to gently push back the announcement. They asked for more time to perform proper due diligence and mitigate risks before making such a significant move. They felt the board needed to weigh in on this level of change, and they were worried about how the announcement might affect donor revenue and staff morale, which were already very low. But they also knew that their primary role as leaders was to consistently demonstrate unwavering commitment, unceasing affirmation, and unending support for every decision the CEO made. They stayed and obeyed because they knew, deep down, that they could not get this type of money working in a nonprofit organization anywhere else in the world.

UNDERSTANDING THE INNER CIRCLE

Both of these fictional case studies underscore what can happen when leaders value loyalty over honesty and affirmation over innovation. Those closest to the leader are often those most trusted, not because of any specific skill set or insight, but because of a history of faithful support. This inner circle is often known for wielding the power of their influence over others, taunting those less faithful with threats of disclosure, knowing that their words would be taken as truth. Their proximity to power often makes them feel more powerful, and their loyalty makes them feel like extensions of the leaders they adore. They are often fiercely protective, pushing against anyone who may share negative words or thoughts about the leader, and deeply devoted, almost to the point of worship. But what the leaders know about them that the inner circle members may not even know about themselves is that they are usually victims of some sort of previous loss or trauma. Sometimes they treat the pastor like their spiritual parent because they have lost a parent. Sometimes they stick with the CEO because they have been betrayed themselves. Dysfunctional loyalty from the inner circle is often a symptom of a deeper wound, one that keeps them tethered to leaders out of fear and not out of faith in God.

In the worst cases, compulsively self-centered leaders intentionally select vulnerable, traumatized, and wounded inner circle members, knowing that any show of love will seal their loyalty for life. They hunt down suffering victims, going out of their way to show demonstrable love that such victims are unlikely to have experienced before, turning them into men and women who will only say yes, no matter what they feel inside. Vows of loyalty easily slip into vows of secrecy to cover up indiscretions, poor decisions, and lies. Before they know it, inner circle members like these can be held accountable for tumultuous sins, ones they may not have even recognized at the time, because they were simply fulfilling their roles as dutiful leaders, confidants, and friends.

This is when loyalty can turn into betrayal for both the leader and those who follow. Leaders who love loyalty will be quick to act when they sense they are being betrayed. Operating out of fear, they can retaliate against others who dare to break the unspoken codes of absolute devotion and protection. Meanwhile, fiercely loyal, traumatized inner circle members are most susceptible to betrayal when the person to whom they cling is the one who turns them away.

Those who choose to speak up about misconduct or who dare to question decisions made by the leader are often shamed, blacklisted, or excommunicated. Such was the case with some of the elders of Mars Hill Church under the leadership of Mark Driscoll.[2] Hidden within the complexities was a simple storyline about leaders who were selected for their loyalty and rejected when they questioned the pastor's authority. But, behind the toxicity of the leadership were men who experienced love and affirmation from Driscoll in ways they never had before. They were loyal because they were loved, and narcissistic leaders can take advantage of that reality.

More commonly, leaders select loyal team members because they just want to get things done. They believe that work gets done faster when everyone is on the same page and that teams are healthiest when nearly everyone agrees. Inner circle members like these are selected for their sameness; they are the people who act and think most like the leaders they serve. Yet, even in these cases, inner circle members are often expected to maintain this sameness across decisions, even when they disagree with the smallest decisions. This goes beyond the mature expectation that internal disagreements would not preclude external unity. The pressure to assimilate and to think like everyone else often triggers people pleasers to please, chameleons to blend in, and bashful people to back down. Even in healthy cultures, leaders who esteem loyalty over any other characteristics can be prone to amplify the pain of traumatized inner circle members who are likely to have suffered similarly in the past.

Whether they are selected for their suffering, for their sameness, or even for their superior skill sets, team members who are closest to the leader are often those most susceptible to the pressure of being loyal above all else. They are likely to see their loyalty as both a duty (part of their profession) and a devotion (part of their personality). This desire to serve a master is part of our human composition, and the willingness to give ourselves in service to another person's success is a noble calling. But the only way that we can help organizations and traumatized populations to thrive is by denying this natural attraction to loyalty and replacing it with steadfast commitment to Christ and his kingdom.

DISLOYAL DISCIPLES

I often wonder why Jesus chose the disciples he did. Without question, his calling was the most difficult one anyone had to fulfill on earth. If anyone needed loyal, faithful people in their corner, surely Jesus did. He needed people he could trust when demons drew near. He needed people he could rely on when Satan tried to thwart his purpose. He certainly needed friends who would stick close when the crowds were quick to walk away. But Jesus did not choose an inner circle the way that an earthly leader would. He chose the weak rather than the strong and started from the margins with people who appeared farthest away. In every way, Jesus chose them according to what he saw for them and what he could do for them, not according to what they saw for themselves or what they could do for him.

Rather than remain loyal to the Lord, every single disciple proved untrustworthy in some way. They were fickle in their affections, shallow in their devotion, and often put their own needs and desires above Jesus. In a context where discipleship required faithfulness, they proved their unfaithfulness over and over, all with varying degrees of shame. Some of the greatest of these examples came through the disciples who were in the inner circle: Peter, James, and John. These three received the calling of Christ together when he met them on the shores (Matthew 4:18-22; Mark 1:16-20; Luke 5:1-11). These were the ones who witnessed Jesus transfigured (Matthew 17:1-9; Mark 9:2-9; Luke 9:28-36). By all estimations, Jesus had earned their loyalty by giving them a place of importance in life they would have never had without him. Jesus gave them prominence and purpose, so much so that James and John believed they had a right to reign with him on the throne (Mark 10:36-37)! Yet these very ones who should have been the most loyal proved themselves to be completely unreliable as Jesus approached the peak of his pain.

They were the only ones invited by Jesus to accompany him in one of his darkest hours as he prayed in the Garden of Gethsemane. His spirit was so heavy with grief that Matthew and Mark record Jesus telling the three disciples that he was "overwhelmed with sorrow to the point of death" and "sorrowful and troubled" (Matthew 26:37-38). Imagine Jesus, the Savior of the world, confessing that he needed the disciples to pray for him! He had asked so very little of them compared to what he gave them, and yet they could not fulfill this one request: to pray and wait on the Lord with him. To the average leader, this would be the straw that breaks the camel's back. If you cannot go with me through the valleys of defeat, you cannot be trusted on the mountains of success. Most leaders would immediately release this group for failure to comply with instructions, failure to support the mission, and failure to fulfill requested duties. They proved, once again, that they could not be loyal, and their faithlessness lasted all the way to betraying him while he was nailed to the cross. How much more disloyal could they be?

The actions of all of the disciples, but especially of those in the inner circle, were grounds for termination and removal from the group. Jesus had every right to let them go knowing that they could not be what he needed them to be. But instead of letting them go, Jesus drew them closer, visited them in their pain, opened their eyes to the truth, and filled them with his Spirit. Why in the world would Jesus do all of that for people who proved repeatedly that they could not be loyal? Perhaps it was because Jesus never needed them to fulfill his calling. Jesus understood that his success was not contingent on their loyalty. Through his relationship with the Father, Jesus demonstrated that dependence on God is more effective than loyalty from people. The deciding factor of his fate came from depending on and drawing strength from the Father more than anyone else in the world. As he modeled this dependence, he was able to show the disciples that dependence is more important than loyalty. If they could learn to depend on God for everything, they would not have to depend on people for anything.

Leadership that depends on loyalty from others runs the risk of being independent from God. When we need people to affirm our decisions and cosign on our actions, we put our mission and calling in their hands and take it away from the hands of God. When they affirm us, we feel valued, and when they betray us, we feel worthless. Leaders who are obsessed with loyalty are desperate for people who can mirror back to them the image they want to portray to the world, even when what is reflected is not real. Like emperors with no clothes, they obsess over team members who will show them images of themselves in superior attire so that they can believe that they have some level of importance. But these leaders often forget what Jesus knew so well: that even the most loyal people, even those closest to you have capacity to betray you. Eventually someone is going to let it slip that the emperor has no clothes. Over time, someone is going to grow tired of protecting a leader's reputation when they know the truth. In cases of sin, the Holy Spirit can be trusted to convict someone so that the truth will ultimately come to the light. When loyalty from people is valued over dependence on God, eventually God will let the loyalty fail in order to protect both the leader and those who follow.

For Jesus, loyalty was reserved for one relationship: the one with the Father. His frequently repeated phrase "I must be about my Father's business" was a guidepost for his ministry, directing what he would and would not do on earth. He refused to be bound to anyone or anything else that might threaten that sense of covenantal loyalty. As a result, Jesus was able to invite us into that sacred covenant, believing that clinging to him automatically meant rejecting the allegiances of the world. This deep and loving commitment is what sets the foundation for marital vows, inviting lovers to "forsake all others, clinging only to each other, till death do them part." The biblical act of clinging simultaneously involves forsaking, understanding that you cannot cling to one covenant without forsaking the other. Perhaps this is why Jesus was clear that you cannot serve God and mammon (Matthew 6:24; Luke 16:13). You cannot covenant with God without simultaneously rejecting the world. As a leader, Jesus invited his disciples into a covenant with God that simultaneously rejected the world for God's glory and their good.

FREEDOM FROM LOYALTY

So, what does it look like to crucify loyalty, free the inner circle, and still get things done? Well, let's just say it's not easy. While there is no single solution to this deep and pervasive challenge, we must first see the problem before we can attempt to solve it. When loyalty is overextended, you'll see it in the way that team members respond to the leader. Here are some questions that can help us uncover whether this is the case:

- Are team members afraid of retribution or backlash for speaking their true thoughts?
- Are they continually asked to support the vision or the leadership without room for question or dissent?
- Is there a sense that those in closest proximity to the person in power are more respected and valued than those who are not, regardless of their positions?
- Is conversation and idea generation halted by people who claim they are the only ones who know what the leader really wants?
- As a leader, do you feel insulted or offended by people who offer views that are different from your own?
- In leadership, do you tend to rely on people who have known you the longest or believe that those closest to you have the best perspective?

If the answer to any of these questions is yes or maybe, there's a chance that loyalty may be too highly regarded in your organization or, as a leader, in your own mind. Fortunately for us, God does not call us to be disloyal but rather to reframe our sense of loyalty so that we can operate more clearly in our callings.

Perhaps the first place to start is by reframing the fear of disagreement. At the core of loyalty is often the spoken or unspoken rule that you must agree with whatever the leader says. In Christian organizations, and especially in the church, we tend to believe that the leader is from God. If that is the case, then it's easy for very loyal people to believe that whatever the leader says is also from God. Whatever the leader does is led by God. Whoever the leader promotes or demotes, honors or shames is the same as coming from God. While this drastic observance of hierarchy is effective in maintaining earthly loyalty out of obedience, it leaves out one critical factor: that leaders are human beings and not God. Leaders, like all people, sin and fall short of God's glory (Romans 3:23). As such, leaders must work hard to help people to hear from God themselves, encouraging them to put faith in leadership in a way that does not take away from deep and abiding faith in God. They can do this by encouraging a level of unity that thrives when there is difference of thought and diversity of opinions.

While loyalty can often stifle creativity by binding people to the ideas of the leader, differing thoughts and opinions can enhance innovation and strengthen leadership. Loyalty to leadership assumes that everyone should think the same. This pressure toward sameness can often smother gifted team members and can be especially harmful toward people who have suffered through abusive relationships. But we can free ourselves and our teams from the bondage of personal loyalty when we make room for people to be themselves, offer their ideas, and enhance the mission with the diversity of their gifts and personalities. Max De Pree said it this way: "We need to give each other the space to grow, to be ourselves, to exercise our diversity. We need to give each other space so that we may both give and receive such beautiful things as ideas, openness, dignity, joy, healing, and inclusion."[3] When people are free from the fear of appearing disloyal, they can experience the joy of bringing their full selves and ideas to their work, causing the entire organization to rise.

This freedom, however, is not a reason for leaders to tolerate insubordination or betrayal. It is not an excuse for maintaining employment or team membership with people who are set on thwarting the organizational mission or intentionally harming the leader. This is why the culture for encouraging differences must be couched in covenant. In many Christian organizations, covenants are designed and signed by individuals who agree to a certain set of terms on how they will be together. As a professor, I remember starting each new course with a class covenant that included ways that we agreed to be a community together. We would set aside time to determine together what was acceptable and what was not, how we wanted to show up and how we wanted to leave, and most importantly, what we were expecting from God. Our lists often included things such as "We agree to silence our phones, only taking calls in cases of emergency" or "We agree to turn to wonder rather than judgment when a perspective is offered that we do not understand." While the details of the covenant might have changed from course to course, we somehow always ended with a closing clause that stated, "We agree to trust God with our time together, believing that when we leave this place, we will be more revived and energized than when we began." Covenants like these helped to set students at ease, reminding them that even classes in practical theology are about God and not solely about the grade.

Covenants establish standards and allow community participants to hold each other accountable for what they agreed to do and how they agreed to be together. However, when traumatized people enter covenants, even ones that help them to become closer to God, there is always a sense of obligation that can turn into manipulation in times of misconduct. If community covenants are to be applied to the whole community, then the leader must also be allowed to be held accountable and corrected when such standards are broken. For example, if an organization struggles with loyalty in a way that stifles new ideas or makes new people feel less important, they might consider a covenant statement like this: "We will encourage creativity and new ideas from all areas of our organization, believing that every vantage point has value." With a statement like this, leaders can help to level the playing field and make it clear that every voice counts. If the pain point is around a fear of backlash for dissention or disagreement, a covenant statement like this could help: "We agree that everyone has the responsibility to report wrongdoing without fear of removal or retaliation." Covenant statements like these allow for organizations to prioritize a set of values that reinforce an individual and collective commitment to God above all else.

But covenants without clear processes mean nothing. A statement of values must be backed by clear processes that prevent abuses of loyalty and protect those who speak the truth. As we consider the stress and traumas of our times, having policies in place will not only help to assure existing

team members that they are safe, they will also help potential new community members to see that you are serious
about their protections. Oftentimes, Christian organizations do not believe they need policies or processes for discipline, knowing that personnel are hired "at will." This
gives them the power to hire and fire whoever they want for
any reason. The same is true for whistleblower protections.
While common in corporate settings, they are often nonexistent in Christian organizations. This makes room for
staff members to be released for naming wrongful behaviors
in leadership and for lay leaders to be excommunicated
from the church or even blacklisted in the community
without any protections. However, when we put policies in
place to protect those who believe they speak the truth, we
can create a safe environment for staff and volunteers to be
free to serve.

Creating a level of safety in policies and procedures does
not mean that we must protect the people who aim to hurt
leaders or their organizations. On the contrary, organizations with such policies can create a check and balance that
allows them to validate what is true and dismiss what is false.
These policies can include room for investigation by the
board members, trustees, or outside council. They can include getting testimonies from participants and hosting
interviews with those closely involved. While the goal would
be that such policies do not have to be used, the mere fact
that they exist can send the message of intentional care and
concern for everyone involved.

EXCHANGING LOYALTY FOR UNITY

Jesus modeled for us what it looks like to experience the unity of the Spirit without the bondage of dysfunctional leadership loyalty. The disciples were anything but loyal, and yet being called by God into a relationship with Christ, they were united in their mission. They were not always on the same page, but they remained united in the body of Christ. When we de-emphasize loyalty to the leader and amplify unity in Christ, we can experience the freedom to be ourselves, to covenant in community, and to operate with processes and procedures that keep everyone safe.

1. When might loyalty toward leadership be helpful? When is it harmful?

2. When was the last time you felt unhealthy pressure to be loyal rather than truthful?

3. Who are the people in the inner circle around you? Do they have the freedom to lovingly correct you or to disagree when they have different ideas?

4. How might God be calling the church toward deeper loyalty to Christ?

5. What is one thing that you can do differently to encourage more freedom in unity on your team?

9

CRUCIFYING SCALE

*From Organizational Growth
to Missional Depth*

GROOMED TO GROW

We cherish systems of scale that allow us to maximize growth and multiply revenue or impact. As humans, we hunger for the results of scale, especially when it means we can get what we want in a better, faster, cheaper way. The Western world especially loves the idea that scaled restaurants allow us to get the same thing in different locations in record time. We crave the consistency of our franchise favorites, expecting our pumpkin spice lattes to taste the same at every Starbucks in every city, every time. We value the uniformity of chain stores, basing our comfort on the predictability of what's inside. We embrace that layer of security that comes from seeing a restaurant, clothing store, or even a church brand that we know and love in cities we've never seen before. While scaling good ideas can be profitable for business owners, it can also prove to be a stabilizing factor for society. Brand recognition lowers cultural ambiguity and consumer anxiety. Predictability and consistency can lead to trust, especially with products and people we know.

This natural desire for growth and reliability has affected every part of our lives, even those areas we would rather ignore. In general, if our first child is happy and healthy, then we're more likely to want another. If our first property sale goes well, we're more likely to want to buy and sell again. When our worship services are reaching traditional standards of bucks (money), butts (attendance), and buildings (paid or low-finance mortgages), we want to scale the method to attract even more. The consumer-driven, Darwinian churn of the profit-focused economy suggests that things that are going well should be scaled up to do more, while things that seem stagnant should be scaled down or die. But as appealing as it may sound, growth is not always necessary or good for every industry or enterprise. Traditional leaders are applauded when they can grow businesses and/or ministries, often with little regard to how it's done. If one's legacy includes numbers that were greater than the start, what happened in the middle to achieve those numbers seems of little consequence. "They started with sixty and grew it to six thousand" appears to be the only thing that matters in a world that believes bigger is better. But what happens when bigger is not better and scale involves scandal?

While growth and scale are often used interchangeably, they mean two different things.[1] Leaders can grow organizations by increasing revenue at the same rate of costs. This is relatively easy to do, especially if you can afford to spend more money to make more money. Leaders who scale organizations do so by increasing revenue more than they increase costs. This leads them to develop more without spending as much. While growth is meaningful, scale is what people desire. In our capitalist society, bigger is only better when it's faster and cheaper. We live for times when demand for what we sell is so high that we *must* scale to meet the market needs. We want scale so badly that we'll even manufacture needs that people don't have. Like the Once-ler in the animated movie *The Lorax*, we'll make up songs and put on shows to make people want things like "thneeds" that no one actually needs. We drive up demand through manipulative marketing and competitive pricing in hopes that we can increase revenue at relatively low operating costs. If we are not intentional, the thirst for scale can make people secondary and put the pursuit of profit over and above anything and anyone else that stands in the way.

While it may sound like this mindset is best practiced by non-Christians, it has long been woven into practices of Christian leaders in search of success as well. In conscious and unconscious ways, we are judged by how well we scale our businesses and ministries, by how well we grow our teams, and by how well we maximize our impact while maintaining or lowering what it costs us to do so.

However well this craving for scale works in capitalism, it does not always fare well when it comes to matters of faith. At times, the subtle and overt worship of scale can cause us to push for more, by any means necessary. It can force us to commercialize and standardize our products, people, and even our worship offerings so that who we are, what we have, and what we do can be easily replicated for others to consume. Whether in business or in ministry, it would behoove Christian leaders to think twice before adapting mindsets of scale, particularly when it comes to the people we serve. Why? Because history proves that what may be profitable for the pocket can do little to soothe the soul.

MOVING ASSEMBLY LINES

> I will build a motor car for the great multitude . . . constructed of the best materials, by the best men to be hired, after the simplest designs that modern engineering can devise . . . so low in price that no man making a good salary will be unable to own one—and enjoy with his family the blessing of hours of pleasure in God's great open spaces.
>
> HENRY FORD (1913)

This audacious vision cast by Henry Ford paved the way for a "better, faster, cheaper" car that was accessible to all Americans. Prior to this vision, automobiles took more than twelve hours to produce and were set at a purchase price ranging between $800 and $1,200. This meant that cars were luxury items for wealthy families who could afford them but beyond reach for much of the working class. In 1913, however, Ford changed the manufacturing industry by testing and deploying the moving assembly line. Instead of trained workers retrieving parts, the assembly line brought the parts to them, creating greater efficiency in time and energy. Workers could get more done in less time, dramatically increasing the number of cars that they could produce. The assembly line increased production as people worked on one or two specific tasks all day, reducing the time it took from more than twelve hours to about ninety minutes from start to finish. The price of Ford's cars became cheaper with streamlined production, lowering the cost of the Model T automobile to about $260. With the entrance of the conveyor belt assembly method, Ford accomplished the task of scaling the auto industry and making the Model T available to more families.[2]

While most people celebrated this dramatic innovation, it did not necessarily benefit everyone. Ford's inspiration came from the conveyor belts at Union Stockyards in Chicago, where meatpacking and processing accelerated on the backs of poor immigrant communities.[3] In this setting, meat disassembly lines were dependent on unskilled workers doing the same job all day long in deplorable environments. While efficiency was high, the conditions were dangerous for vulnerable employees, and the industry essentially wiped local butchers off the map. "Technological innovations were made, monopolies were created, labor clashed with tycoons, economies were transformed, environments destroyed, and the American consumer's relationship to food was forever changed."[4] The appeal of scaled mass production proved to be more valuable than what it cost communities and even society at large.

Similarly at Ford, workers who found joy in assembling a complete automobile now found themselves robotically doing the same thing all day, and small local car manufacturers were forced to shut down. Ford managed to curb some effects by offering higher wages and shorter shifts, but it did not change the monotony that came with working the assembly line. While many people appreciated the accessibility of the Model T, there were others who were not satisfied with having what everyone else had. They wanted something better, faster, and cheaper, but they also wanted something that was high quality, unique, and had character. Companies such as General Motors jumped on this desire, and by the 1920s they began to offer more flexible pricing and a wider variety of cars through trade-ins, closed car models, annual model design changes, and more.[5] They capitalized on the fact that the Ford assembly line only worked for a fixed model, while consumers wanted variety and change. Ford attempted to solve this challenge by creating a variation on the Model T, but many people felt that it was too late. The innovation of scale worked for a season, until the market wanted more dynamism than assembly line production could meet.

FEARLESS FACTORIES

> I am not merely satisfied in making money for myself,
> for I am endeavoring to provide employment for hun-
> dreds of women of my race.
>
> MADAME C. J. WALKER (1914)

One such driver of this Model T Ford was self-made millionaire Madam C. J. Walker. Her success came from the
scale of hair products for Black women that simultaneously
resulted in scale that featured increased jobs, income, education, and self-sufficiency. Women craved the hair products
that made them feel beautiful when society said otherwise.
They admired the miraculous story of Sarah Breedlove, an
orphaned domestic worker, who became Madam C. J.
Walker, the millionaire business mogul. During a time
when Black women had few models of what it looked like
to grow businesses, Walker beat the odds by creating space
for herself and others to scale through products and processes that elevated them.

She and like-minded contemporaries, including Annie
Turnbo Malone, found that both economic and social scale
can grow together. As they found better, cheaper ways to
manufacture their products, they also discovered new ways
to employ thousands of Black women, educating them in
schools and colleges and deploying them into the workforce in ways that no other industry would allow at that
time. Their success in scaling products, businesses, and jobs
for women within their communities gave them leverage
for philanthropy and generosity that inspired movements

toward equity in race and gender. Whether advocating for women to vote or contributing to causes that advanced equal rights for Black communities, it is clear that, like Ford, both Walker and Malone saw their businesses as tools to advance society as a whole instead of just increasing profits for themselves. While both businesses did extremely well for their times, they both faced challenges in sustaining operations amid the Great Depression, in managing through personal losses, and in leadership succession.

FAST-FOOD REVOLUTION

Around the same time, a similar story grew from the scale of one of America's most iconic foods: hamburgers. The earliest scaled production of fast-food hamburgers started with White Castle in Wichita, Kansas, in 1921. This was arguably the first food chain in America and took pride in the concept of little burgers, later called "sliders," that consumers could "buy by the sack."[6] The stores managed to increase production and keep up with demand through assembly line kitchens and practical innovations like paper napkins for customers and hats for employees.[7] Ten years later, founder Walter Anderson and his partner, E. W. Ingram, had increased to 116 locations in eleven states. But this level of scale did not match the level of later competitors like the McDonald's franchise.

The vigor and pace of growth for McDonald's was so great that one 1995 study found that more people recognized the double arches than they did the Christian cross.[8] This simple vision of providing better, faster, cheaper food in 1940 was birthed by two brothers, Richard and Maurice (Mac) McDonald, who were eager to find ways to speed their production after the success of their first restaurant. They discovered they could do so by offering fewer options and preparing items in an assembly line fashion, similar to what White Castle was doing. They could serve even more people when items were prepared ahead of time and kept warm until customers arrived. But, arguably, it was not until Ray Kroc took over the business in 1961 that McDonald's began to experience tremendous growth.

In many ways, Kroc did for the fast-food industry in the 1960s what Ford did for the automobile industry in the early 1900s: he streamlined operations in such a clinical and precise way that every item was produced the same way every time, regardless of where their products were located. This was a deliberate decision with significant costs, both intended through profits and unintended in its effects on others. For this reason, White Castle opted not to pay the cost of scale to preserve their connection with customers and employees. Fourth-generation CEO, Lisa Ingram, defended the decision not to pursue more, stating, "You have to give up control and you have to give up the ownership of the customer and the ownership of the team member . . . and that's just not something that we have ever really been interested in doing."[9] As McDonald's took defined steps toward expansion, White Castle owners took clear steps toward control, and both decisions carried consequences.

In each of these cases, the ideas for scale arose from a need to make something people wanted more accessible in faster, cheaper, more efficient ways. The original desire to grow was what catalyzed scale, and the fact that each business still impacts consumers in some way today proves that it is possible to scale, fail, and scale again to ensure evergreen profits. But to presume that these stories can be anyone's story would be a significant misstep. The mechanics at Ford during the introduction of the moving assembly line would likely say that scale cost them their passion for work. Some historians might argue that overwhelming growth of business for Malone and Walker cost them their marriages, affected their children, and made succession even more difficult. McDonald's owners and workers might say that scale came at the expense of local creativity and expression. Since these are all free market businesses, society would say if anyone doesn't like it, they can go somewhere else or support another business. But for leaders considering when and how to scale, we cannot ignore what these stories tell us: that scale always comes with a cost, no matter how much profit shows up in the ledger.

A BETTER, FASTER, MORE ACCESSIBLE GOSPEL

A far more complex and difficult story exists around scaling churches and ministries. The marketplace norms of supply and demand make growth and scale an expected part of consumerism but a more tenuous part of charity and faith.

On one hand, the popularity of megachurches, exponential church planting, and multi-site ministries proves that it is possible to grow ministry beyond the limits of the four walls. Advancing swiftly with devoted givers and influencers who extend the church's brand, megachurches of two thousand or more weekly attenders remain an attractive worship model in America.[10] They tend to draw members who are looking for more vibrant, diverse, and younger experiences, while smaller churches struggle to keep up with the trends. Similarly, multi-campus or multi-site churches are growing in popularity where the brand or personality of the church can be extended to more than one location. Like franchises, this model provides the consistency of a popular experience to be extended in multiple cities while still adhering to the core personality of the leader and brand promise.

Church planting movements continue to grow as well, emphasizing what David Garrison defines as "rapidly multiplying indigenous churches planting churches that sweep across a people group or population segment."[11] The fast pace of developing local house churches matches the rapid acceleration of local Bible translation, making it possible to advance multiple elements at one time. While the general American narrative is that church attendance is decreasing, these unique segments would say that ministry is increasing as large churches grow, popular churches franchise, and church planting turns Bible translation into Bible engagement and community growth. If this is the case, why wouldn't every church want to become a mega-, multi-, or movement church? If the gospel is a commodity that everyone will always need for every generation, then why wouldn't we want pastors to apply principles from the likes of Ford, Walker, Malone, and Kroc? Perhaps the answer is the same in the church as it is in business: because scale always comes with cost, no matter what profit shows up in the ledger or what people show up in the pews.

While businesses might excuse people being treated poorly or workers being sacrificed for the sake of scale, Christian organizations must argue otherwise.

THE SCARS OF SCALE

Let's reiterate the fact that scale and growth can be good. In fact, scale and growth can come from God! But this truth must be balanced with the biblical reality that bigger is not always better, faster is not always faithful, cheaper is not always effective, and the ends do not always justify the means. In other words, while growth and scale are not bad in and of themselves, the motivations behind them are what matter most. This is especially true when it comes to the way that scale and growth affect the people we lead. Whether we like it or not, people become more expendable when a better, faster, cheaper business outcome becomes our only goal. In these cases, you'll hear leaders say things like, "Swim or get out of the pool, row or get off the boat, pee or get off the pot." The pursuit of scale and growth means that anyone who cannot go at the pace of the desired growth is no longer valuable or needed. There is no room for questions, no space for doubt, no time for hesitation, and no tolerance for a slower pace. In spaces where growth and scale are the only object, it makes sense that whatever does not bring a return can be removed, even if what is removed are people going through burnout, trauma, stress, or personal difficulty. When the business or ministry train moves too quickly, those who are not securely on board will be left behind or, worse, get run over.

Granted, it is true that not everyone is cut out for the fast-paced, rapid acceleration of growing businesses or scaling ministries. But might it also be true that Christian leaders who run such organizations should have an ethos and motivation that is different from their non-Christian counterparts? While the world couldn't care less about the effects of scale on the people who serve, God's kingdom would say otherwise. If God cares deeply for everyone, regardless of their contribution to the church or society, how might Christian leaders do the same while growing and scaling organizations? Since scale is typically costly, leaders will do well to consider the real costs and evaluate the true profit potential before proceeding with accelerated growth that could take us farther away from where we ultimately long to be.

SCALING WITH SACRED INTENTIONS

There is one primary motivation that accelerates secular growth and scale in commerce more than anything else. This one motivation is responsible for some of the greatest growth curves our world has ever seen and simultaneously responsible for every single related downfall. The motivation?

Greed. *Greed* can be summarized as an intense longing for something that has yet to be received. Whether it's focused on money or power or influence or fame, greed is dangerous because it is insatiable. Gordon Gekko, the business executive from the 1987 movie *Wall Street,* coined the iconic phrase "Greed is good, greed is right, greed works."[12] However, once you get some of what you want, greed leaves you wanting more. It is never satisfied with higher profits. It wants the highest profits possible. It is not content with millions impacted by ministry. It wants to reach billions.

When scale and growth are good for consumers or good for charity or good for the spread of the gospel, greed can turn what is good into evil at the tip of the hat. With greed, leaders don't know when to stop. Bernie Madoff is a prime example: greed punched him a ticket aboard the runaway train to ruin; he and others like him didn't know how to turn it off or how to quell the desires for more.[13] Greed causes people to be sacrificed in the pursuit of what is good and can turn a good idea into a spiral of bad results. This most heinous of desires harms more than just profits and outcomes and legacy. Greed ruins and hurts people, causing them to lose what is lasting in pursuit of what is temporary, as almost every scaling hero can proclaim.

Again, it's important to note that scale and growth are in and of themselves not bad, but they must stem from the right motivations to cause the least harm. For this reason, the greedy motivation for more must be crucified for divine growth and scale to be resurrected for God's glory. The ministry of Jesus attests to this fact. In a crowd of several thousands, Jesus proceeded to have two conversations: one with the crowds and another with his disciples. To the crowds, he spoke in parables, but to the disciples, he spoke in warnings. On this occasion recorded in Luke 12, Jesus was invited to respond to a demand from the crowd but turned it around as a teachable moment for his disciples as well.

> Someone in the crowd said to him, "Teacher, tell my brother to divide the inheritance with me."
>
> Jesus replied, "Man, who appointed me a judge or an arbiter between you?" Then he said to them, "Watch out! Be on your guard against all kinds of greed; life does not consist in an abundance of possessions." (Luke 12:13-15)

In a gathering of so many people that Luke said they started to trample each other, the concern of one man was for the inheritance that he felt was owed to him. He did not cry out for ways to live life with more meaning. He did not even cry out to Jesus on behalf of the sick or dying, as many others did. No, in this moment, the only thing this man could think to ask the Messiah in a crowd full of people was for money, land, or whatever else his family had left behind.

Jesus may have been agitated by this demand, coming to him as a statement instead of a question, but what he did after addressing the man was most telling. He turned to his disciples and used this moment to teach them about greed. He urged them to be on guard against all kinds of greed, treating greed like a virus that is easily spread from one to another. He warned them to watch out for this tactic of the enemy, not only because of what greed does to the heart of humans but also because of the effect greed has on the meaning of life. Jesus was urging them and us to be careful not to evaluate our lives by what we have, how fast we grow, or how much we accumulate. He underscored this warning in a parable to the crowd, ending with the fact that what we save for ourselves means nothing if we are not "rich toward God" (Luke 12:21).

Notice that Jesus does not condemn possessions in the parable, and he does not warn his disciples against having an inheritance or anything that amounts to wealth. The rebuke in this text is specifically about the motive for the wealth and the aim for the possessions. In place of greed that pushes us to want more, Jesus invites us to long for purpose. In place of hoarding possessions for ourselves, Jesus invites us to give generously to God and others for God's glory.

Now, some may use this text to defend the scaling of ministry through multiple campuses or the growth of a business to multiple countries. They may claim they are growing and scaling because that is what God wants from them and whatever they make, they give away to those in need. To summarize Jesus' response to the greedy man, who are we to judge? Our role as leaders is not to judge the motives of others but to regularly assess our own. One ministry may grow with good motives and another with poor ones, but only God can judge. One business may scale with intentions to give while another scales with intentions to hoard, but only God knows the intentions of the heart. For this reason, Christian leaders must be willing to regularly crucify the intentions and motives of our hearts, not for fear of man but for fear of God. At the end of our days, we want our ministries and businesses and the organizations we lead to be abundant in purpose and in glory to God, not simply in profits and self-gratification.

STEWARDSHIP OVER SCALE

The work of assessing our motives with growth and scale will take intentionality, discipline, accountability, and time. It will not be easy, and there will certainly be times when growth and scale will be called into question. But if we are willing to continue the journey, we will find healing for our own leadership that results in healing for those we serve. Here are a few ways to keep moving in this direction:

1. *Understand the seasons.* The book of Ecclesiastes is clear: "There is a time for everything, and a season for every activity under the heavens" (Ecclesiastes 3:1). There are times when growth accelerates and times when it stalls. There are times when churches buy buildings and times when they must sell. Do not count your success only on the seasons of scale; rather, count success in the stewardship of what you have today. At times, it will be more godly and courageous to scale back than it will be to scale up. In times of great success, you will need to know when to keep going and when

to stop, understanding the difference between what you can do and what you should do. All that is good doesn't need to be aggrandized, and all that is grand doesn't necessarily remain. When you trust God for the seasons of your organization, you will put your hope in faithful stewardship over increasing scale.

2. *Clarify your why.* Ask yourself and others why you must scale and grow now, and take an assessment of what will happen if you don't. Ensure that your motive for scale is rooted in your organizational purpose and that the benefits will apply to more than just the immediate stakeholders. Articulate this why early and often so that everyone understands the significance of the goal.

3. *Understand what is being scaled . . . and what is not.* In churches, it's easy to focus on growing brand and voice over the reach of the gospel. In businesses, it's easy to believe that the products and services are being scaled over the people soon to be reached. But if motives are to be kept in check, it will be critical to clarify that ministries grow by God's urging and invitation so that people may grow with God. Businesses led by Christian leaders grow and scale to exponentially increase impact, no matter what products or services are being expanded. Leading with clarity on impact as the primary outcome will keep the peripheral indicators from becoming central.

4. *Make room for collective discernment.* Allow those who will carry the burden of scale with you to give voice to the timing, direction, and process of incremental growth. While leadership does not have to be a democracy, making room for various voices to contribute lessens the pressure on the leader. Collective discernment and engagement also make it easier to ask staff members to take on additional work or to assume new roles because they've been empowered in the process. This may not be ideal for every decision for growth and scale, but the sooner you can involve and bring people along with you, the better equipped they will be to serve.

5. *Communicate the costs.* If scale always comes with a cost, then the best we can do is to communicate that to people we serve. Costs may include the reduction or addition of new roles, the reorienting of existing work, or even moving to a new location. No matter what the cost may be, people who have endured trauma are best served when they are aware as opposed to being kept in the dark. Timing is still everything, but communication is key to make sure that organizations are prepared for what growth and scale will mean for everyone involved.

6. *Emphasize well-being.* It may feel impossible to communicate well-being when an organization is scaling up or down, especially if it serves to manipulate acceptance of a new direction. But recognizing that work is

a part of our lives and not the whole will help in communicating directions of scale and growth. In times of scaling up, emphasizing well-being can look like giving staff a few extra days off after enormous growth. In times of scaling down, emphasizing well-being can be as simple as the offer of counseling and job transition support through professional or community partners. When we take the time to care for the whole person, we invest in our organizations and in our own integrity as well.

As attractive as it may be to grow your organization to exponential heights, the calling for godly leaders is to steward what you have with right motives. Whether stewardship means increasing or decreasing, scaling up or scaling down, the key is to crucify false motives of greed, pride, and selfishness so that what is resurrected reflects the generosity, selflessness, and grace of God.

PART 3

THE

PROMISE

10

RESURRECTING HEALING AND HOPE

The Value of the Dream

Come, let's dream together! Do you remember what it feels like to dream? Often we start by closing our eyes. This step helps us to shut off the limitations of what is around in the moment. It helps to open a pathway of seeing with our minds what cannot currently be perceived with our eyes. Then, we typically relax our bodies. In sleep, it's usually easier to relax the body than it is the mind, though the two go hand in hand. We command our muscles to loosen around our faces, our necks, our shoulders, our arms, abs, and legs. Eventually, the body will start to coach the mind, sometimes into a state of sleep and sometimes into a place of peaceful contemplation. Once our eyes succeed in blocking out the pressure around us, our bodies cooperate with the position of rest, and our minds finally give up on trying to process it all, we are properly positioned to dream.

When we dream, we can see what has yet to be seen. We can feel the emotions often hidden beneath the surface of our lives, both good and bad, giving us hope and making us afraid. Our dreams are companions to creativity. They help us to think outside of our limitations to solve problems, design strategies, and imagine new things. With dreams, we can soar above the proverbial trees to see the forest from a new perspective. We give ourselves permission to conceive of new possibilities devoid of our typical hesitations and anxieties. Even when our fears materialize in our dreams, overwhelming us with dread or the anticipation of pain, dreams still remind us that visions are as real as we allow them to be.

Dreaming is an important part of a healthy life and, therefore, an important part of healthy leadership. Leaders who regularly dream have the capacity to create new possibilities. They are better equipped to solve problems, imagine new futures, and envision alternative options. When leaders understand how to dream, they can operate beyond the boundaries that confine them and push past the barriers that hold themselves and others back. They have the capacity to see beyond: beyond the challenges, beyond the past, even and especially beyond themselves. But if a leader forgets how to dream, they can cut off the circulation that fuels the future. Without a leader's dreams, there is no life flow to pump the heart of the organization and no aspiration with potential to become reality. If you, my fellow leader, cannot conjure a vision of how you want to lead and of who you want to be, you may never fully activate God's power invested within you.

Believe it or not, the ability to dream is critical for imagining a new way of leading when everything around you looks the exact same. Dreaming of a new way of leading requires a very similar process to the way you prepare for dreams as you sleep. You must be able to shut off the images that are before you to see the images and realities that are beyond you. You have to loosen the tensions of muscle memory that keep you in the pattern of doing what you've always done. You must allow these slackened muscles to speak to your mind, giving yourself permission to move without the pressure to make sense or meaning. In order to dream, you must learn to let go of what you see, how you feel, and of what you think you know. This is what crucifixion is ultimately about: it is the process of preparing for a dream of resurrection hope. This is what it will take to try on new leadership styles and abilities. The way to give yourself fully to God through the crucifixion of what you see is to embrace the dream of a resurrected life to lead in ways others have never seen. It takes courage to dream because dreaming sets you apart from what others believe is possible. While dreaming is necessary for life and for leadership, the truth is, dreaming is risky.

RISKY RELEASE

It does not cost much to envision a better way to serve others. In fact, it is rewarding to imagine new leadership methods that advance the work of teams and individuals. The cost of dreaming for leaders comes in what must be released. Throughout this journey, we've talked about what must be crucified within us in order for Christlike leadership to be resurrected through us. We've tried to imagine the joy of resurrection, knowing that whatever must die is despised. But to be faithful to ourselves and to the process, we must acknowledge the fact that it's hard to let go, even when things are harmful. Whether power or ego, performance or perfection, it is hard to release the habits and tendencies that come naturally to us. In loyalty, speed, and scale, it may be easy to believe the principles in our minds but harder to dislodge the actions from our hearts. It takes work and intentionality to decide to let go of something you know in a way that makes room for the unknown. What makes this even scarier is the fact that releasing a way of leading and embracing something new does not always guarantee success. You may reframe your understanding of power and find yourself without a job. You could adjust your perceptions of performance and find people who hold that against you. The risk of release is not simply the process of letting go; it's also the ambiguity of the results.

Moreover, release carries risk because it requires sacrifice. In the same way that crucifixion is synonymous with sacrifice, letting go of old ways of leading is consistent with sacrificing old means and methods. Godly leadership requires, even boldly demands, that we sacrifice something for the good of the whole. Or better stated, someone: ourselves. Renowned leadership expert John Maxwell declares

it this way: "A leader must give up to go up."[1] They must give
of themselves and sacrifice their own desires to ensure that
the teams they serve and the organizations they lead can
succeed. For Maxwell, this was an irrefutable law. When it
comes to dreaming, sacrifice and release are indisputable
steps to resurrect a vision of healthy leadership. But once
again, much easier said than done.

We may talk about the principles of sacrifice, but the
ideas become harder to execute as society becomes more
focused on gains. Even in church ministry, we see greater
emphasis and pressure placed on what we gain as opposed
to what we are willing to give for the sake of the gospel. Very
few, for example, would respond to an altar call inviting
them to risk their lives, give up their money, and sacrifice
their relationships for Christ. Instead, we focus on gaining
a church family, increasing in faith, and receiving heavenly
rewards. While both the risks and rewards are true, we try
to win others by emphasizing what they can receive and put
less emphasis on what the gospel requires that they give up.
Even faith-based philanthropy prides itself on assessing the
missional return on investment. Many generous believers
wonder, *If my financial investments in the world are based on
what I get in return, how much more should I carefully consider my
tithe, my offering, and my donation to Christian organizations
based on what can be gained in return?* While they may not
necessarily look for material returns, they long to see increased impact resulting from what they contribute. Very
few, if any, are willing to invest in ministries that will

decrease over time or shrink with added funding, even if it's the right thing to do.

The world around us would rather increase, but the gospel invites us to do the opposite. At the core of crucifixion is sacrifice, but at the core of capitalism is gain. How can we lead in the tensions between the world and the gospel without losing everything? Perhaps the answer comes down to the anatomy of a dream.[2] According to psychologists, dreams are comprised of both memories from the past and imaginations of the future. One scientist suggested that "our ability to constructively remember the past underlies our capacity to creatively imagine the future."[3]

In other words, we cannot effectively dream unless we are willing to strategically remember. If we are willing to take an impartial look at our past leadership, we might be able to discern what must be released in order to imagine what more could be gained. This is where resurrected leadership lives. It thrives in the intersection of loss for the sake of gain and individual sacrifice for the sake of collective reward. Resurrected leadership thrives when we are willing to die to ourselves so that Christ may be lifted in us. In the words of John the Baptist, "He must become greater; I must become less" (John 3:30). The "must" in this equation suggests that there is no other way. If Christ is to live in me, then something in me must die. If Christ is to resurrect transformative leadership through me, then my old views of leadership must also die. The purpose of crucifying leadership is therefore intricately linked to the ebb and flow of decrease/increase, release/receive, let go/let come, and ultimately of life/death. The differential between these two forces can only be determined by the power of the Holy Spirit.

LEARNING TO LEAD LOW

There is clearly no silver bullet that will make leadership suddenly healthy and humble, but there is one key factor without which all leadership fails: the person of the Holy Spirit. By God's Spirit, leaders can reflect on what must be released from the past to receive what can be gained for the future, but it will not be the same for us all. As we've already seen for issues of power and ego, what one person needs may differ from another and will require different calibrations of loss and gain. We must be guided by the Holy Spirit to know what to ramp up and what to tone down. While our unique recipes for renewed leadership may vary, what can be true for all leaders striving to become more like Christ is the fact that crucifixion invites us to lead low. By leading low, I mean leading from a position of servitude instead of superiority, locating ourselves at the foot of the cross. Unless we lower ourselves before God and people, we can never truly serve. And unless we serve, we can never truly lead. Some scholars call this servant leadership, but if we are truly willing to let things die in crucifixion so that Christ may be resurrected in us, perhaps a better phrase is redemptive leadership.

Crucified leadership resurrects a truer vision of Christlike leadership within us that is both redemptive and healing.

It redeems the value in teams that can be lost when leaders obsess over the wrong things. It buys back what is stolen when leaders succumb to the temptations that rob their souls and strip integrity from others. The redemption of crucifixion is the fact that what dies in Christ is not simply resurrected in the same state but is raised with even greater glory.

This mystery of dying in one form and being raised in another is what Paul talked about when he spoke of our own death and resurrection at the coming of Christ. Paul was responding to questions about whether we will be resurrected in the same bodies when we die or not. To this he says, "So will it be with the resurrection of the dead. The body that is sown is perishable, it is raised imperishable; it is sown in dishonor, it is raised in glory; it is sown in weakness, it is raised in power; it is sown a natural body, it is raised a spiritual body" (1 Corinthians 15:42-44).

While he was explicitly talking about our bodily death and resurrection, the same principles can be applied to the death and resurrection of leadership. We may grieve the loss of what must be crucified, but we can rejoice in knowing that what is resurrected in its place is better than what was there before. When we allow our plans to die in Christ, for example, what is resurrected is not the same plan but a better plan for the glory of God and the good of the people. When we surrender our worldly tactics and strategies to God, what he resurrects in us is far better than what we could imagine for ourselves. And the only way this happens is when it is infused with power by the

Holy Spirit. For when we are made low by God's Spirit in our postures toward God and people, we can lead and live at unimaginable heights.

DREAMING THE IMPOSSIBLE DREAM

So, let's return to dreaming together. By the power of the Holy Spirit, we've been given tools to help us reflect on the past to imagine a resurrected future. But what does it really look like, leading from crucifixion with hopes of resurrection glory? Here are a few examples to inspire your imagination.

Crucifying power: A path for the powerless.

> Then Esther sent this reply to Mordecai: "Go, gather together all the Jews who are in Susa, and fast for me. Do not eat or drink for three days, night or day. I and my attendants will fast as you do. When this is done, I will go to the king, even though it is against the law. And if I perish, I perish." (Esther 4:15-16)

The story of Queen Esther is hard to forget. But before we rest on her traditional traits of beauty or sexual appeal, perhaps the greatest characteristics of this queen were her courage and intentionality in balancing the weights of power. On one hand, she had a position of power as someone with access to the king. She was named queen after Vashti was banished and took on the position of influence as Xerxes's new wife. She was the only one who was able to woo him and, therefore, enjoyed some measure of his pleasure. But on the other hand, she had been robbed of her personal power. As part of the king's pursuit to find a new woman, she was abducted from her homeland, forced to perform sexual acts for the king, and convinced by her uncle, with no mention of a living father or mother, to keep quiet about her heritage. In this regard, she was powerless, and we could argue that even though she eventually came into a position of power, she struggled in her ability to walk in it. She needed affirmation from Mordecai to exercise the authority of her position. She needed the encouragement of her people who would willingly pray for her. Because of her willingness to rise up in power despite her lack of power, she found courage to risk her life for this moment of leadership and calling.

Esther fuels our dreams of what it looks like to walk in the balance of God-given power. For those who struggle with feelings of powerlessness, her story tells of a God who reminds us of who we are in him. For those who inhabit positions of power, her story urges us to steward that power, access, and influence for those who need it most. Above all, Esther reminds us that balancing God-given power takes risk and might cause us to lose our positions, our possessions, and even our lives. But with the strength of a praying community and the power of the Holy Spirit, the risk will be worth the reward.

Crucifying ego: A cure for the conceited.

Even if I should choose to boast, I would not be a fool, because I would be speaking the truth. But I refrain, so no one will think more of me than is warranted by what I do or say, or because of these surpassingly great revelations. Therefore, in order to keep me from becoming conceited, I was given a thorn in my flesh, a messenger of Satan, to torment me. (2 Corinthians 12:6-7)

Paul had every right to be boastful. His background was enough to make any religious leader jealous: he was the top of his Pharisaical class, had followed all the customs of Rabbinic law, was a Roman citizen, and was zealous in his devotion to God. He was proud of his path and committed to doing everything right. And then he met Jesus who turned it all around. His encounter with Christ on the Damascus road in Acts 9 changed everything about Paul. His mission was changed from zeal for the law to zeal for the gospel. His audience changed from a selective focus on the Jews to a broader focus on the Gentiles. Even his posture changed from teacher to student, gleaning first from Ananias and then from the other apostles. The one thing that did not seem to change was Paul's ego. It appears that conversion to Christ did little to tame his natural pride. But God intervened to temper his arrogance in a way that allowed for greater glory to him. In this passage in 2 Corinthians, Paul spoke of the thorn that was sent by God. While it tormented him and felt more like a demonic attack than a divine gift, it was the tool God used to keep him from becoming too conceited.

The consolation we have in Paul's story is the fact that God will always step in to temper what gets out of control. Whether through thorns or demotions, through closed doors or close friends, when we surrender our lives and leadership to him, God will find a way to keep our egos exactly where they need to be. This is important to understand, especially when the world applauds egos that are out of control. In a culture where shamelessness is a superpower of its own, we can heed Paul's example by boasting in our weaknesses, confessing our guilt, and leaning on the supernatural power of God to regulate our egos in the right times and places.

Crucifying speed: A pace for purpose.

> (It takes eleven days to go from Horeb to Kadesh Barnea by the Mount Seir road.) In the fortieth year, on the first day of the eleventh month, Moses proclaimed to the Israelites all that the LORD had commanded him concerning them. . . . The LORD our God said to us at Horeb, "You have stayed long enough at this mountain. . . . See, I have given you this land. Go in and take possession of the land the LORD swore he would give to your fathers—to Abraham, Isaac and Jacob—and to their descendants after them." (Deuteronomy 1:2-3, 6, 8)

It could have taken them eleven days. If they were willing to follow and willing to fight, if they had proven to God and to themselves that they would be faithful to heed the directions of the one who brought them out of Egypt, they could have gotten to the Promised Land in eleven days. But instead, because of a generation's disobedience, God took them through the wilderness for forty years (Deuteronomy 1:2, 35-36). Moses expounded on this reality in Numbers when he described the consequences of the sin of rebellion. Rather than believing the spies who brought a good report about the land, they tried to stone them, complaining against Moses and against God. Their punishment was that the generation of unbelievers would never see the Promised Land. They were subjected to forty years in the wilderness, one year for each day the spies explored the land, as a reminder that God was against them (Numbers 14:34). A journey that could have been remarkable in its speed became memorable because of its years of languish through varied lands. While it was clearly God's desire to get them there, he proved in this act that he cared more about who they became than how quickly they got there.

The journey in the wilderness is not always about sin. Sometimes it's about the principles and practices God wants to instill within us. God uses the wilderness to remind us that time matters differently to God. While we may see speed as the best way to get to the destination, God sees the journey of formation as more valuable. Our impulse to arrive as quickly as possible can be tempered by the reality that God will make the destination worth our wait. His unfailing love for the Israelites and his faithfulness to the covenant can keep us patiently waiting for his move.

Crucifying performance: An antidote for achievers.

> But Martha was distracted by all the preparations that had to be made. She came to him and asked, "Lord, don't you care that my sister has left me to do the work by myself? Tell her to help me!"

"Martha, Martha," the Lord answered, "you are worried and upset about many things, but few things are needed—or indeed only one. Mary has chosen what is better, and it will not be taken away from her." (Luke 10:40-42)

Martha's story is the life that centered around what she could do for others. She cooked for others, maintained the household on behalf of others, and regularly provided for the needs of others when they came to stay. Perhaps it was her performance of these deeds that made her home so appealing to Jesus. Martha, her sister Mary, and their brother Lazarus were friends of the Savior and he visited them on several occasions. But on one of these occasions, when Jesus and the disciples met at their house, Martha's performance took center stage. Forgetting why and for whom she performed, Martha found herself frustrated by the lack of support around her. She was doing her best to provide food without any help from Mary. She was trying to serve with superior hospitality with no help from the other woman in the house. Yet when Martha brought her complaints to the Lord, he chided her gently with a reminder of what really mattered. Honoring her words and calling her by name was a sign of his care for who she was over and above what she could do for him. Jesus offered Martha another way of seeing her performance, not simply as the focus of her existence, but as an offering to Christ.

Surrounded by performance-based leadership and culture, it is easy for us to believe that we are only as good as the things we do and only as strong as our last performance. We can tout our achievements when we think they make us matter more or might render a greater level of applause. But just as Jesus saw Martha for who she was, her story is a reminder that Jesus sees us as well. He sees and appreciates us for who we are above anything good we could possibly do. Jesus invites us to be with him in a way that makes us want to use our gifts for him as our sole audience. When we do this, we recognize that God's pleasure in us stems from who we are in him.

Crucifying perfection: A realistic relationship.

> Have mercy on me, O God, according to your unfailing love; according to your great compassion blot out my transgressions. Wash away all my iniquity and cleanse me from my sin. . . . Create in me a pure heart, O God, and renew a steadfast spirit within me. Do not cast me from your presence or take your Holy Spirit from me. (Psalm 51:1-2, 10-11)

David was far from perfect. Sure, he was better than Saul and anointed over his brothers. It's true that he was a dynamic king and one that God considered to be "a man after my own heart" (1 Samuel 13:14; Acts 13:22). But in all of his near perfect worship and in the midst of his almost faultless leadership, there were key moments of significant sin.

There was the sin of not dealing with the rape of his daughter Tamar, which lead to a battle between two of his sons (2 Samuel 13). There was the sin of counting the troops without God's consent, which led to the destruction of seventy thousand men (2 Samuel 24:15). On top of this was the sin against Uriah when he had him killed in battle and the sin against Bathsheba when he raped her. For someone obsessed with the perfection of everything and power to do anything, this could have been the perfect time to cover things up. But when he was confronted by Nathan and reminded of his crimes, David confessed and begged for God's mercy. The child born from this nonconsensual union would die, but David would be spared and given the opportunity to make things right. It is with this posture that he penned Psalm 51, repenting of his sins and begging God for his presence. David's desire for union with God reinforced his priority of relationship over rightness. He would rather be in relationship with God than to be right in his own eyes. As a result, God honored his legacy through the birth of Solomon, Bathsheba's son, who would become the heir to the throne.

Speaking to us through history, David implores us to put righteousness above rightness and relationship with God over the justification of ourselves. For those who strive for perfection or think, by chance, they have arrived, David says, "Surely [you were] sinful at birth, sinful from the time [your] mother conceived [you]" (Psalm 51:5). Perfectionists have been betrayed by our sinful nature, but through crucifixion, we can resurrect perfect union with Christ with the power of the Holy Spirit. This union is the only thing we should strive to perfect because it is the only way to attain any earthly level of excellence as we lead.

Crucifying loyalty: The fruitfulness of faithfulness.

> "Look," said Naomi, "your sister-in-law is going back to her people and her gods. Go back with her." But Ruth replied, "Don't urge me to leave you or to turn back from you. Where you go I will go, and where you stay I will stay. Your people will be my people and your God my God. Where you die I will die, and there I will be buried. May the LORD deal with me, be it ever so severely, if even death separates you and me." When Naomi realized that Ruth was determined to go with her, she stopped urging her. (Ruth 1:15-18)

There was arguably no one more loyal and faithful in Scripture than Ruth. She clung to Naomi, even when she had good reasons to let her go. As a Moabite woman, Ruth had no obligation to remain with her Israelite mother-in-law. She could have gone back to her people and found a new path, either through marriage or through widowhood to be cared for by others. But her loyalty to Naomi was a sign of her loyalty to God. She was willing to release her lineage, her people, and her gods to take on Naomi's lineage, people, and the one true God. This act of devotion would prove to be fruitful, but not without cost. While Ruth's story eventually leads her to marry Boaz, the family's kinsman redeemer (Ruth 3:9), it also leads to an obscure sense of being overlooked by the woman to whom she was most devoted. After Boaz married Ruth, they bore a son named Obed who would be the grandfather of King David. This miraculous connection came from Ruth's faithfulness to Naomi, but upon the birth of the child, the text suggests that people celebrated Obed as Naomi's son. Some scholars suggest that Naomi raised him as her own. Others say that this was in reference to Naomi's chosen lineage and role in connecting Ruth to Boaz. Whether Ruth was venerated by Naomi or not, her loyalty to God proved more meaningful than any faithfulness to people on earth.

The difficulty of human loyalty is the painful existence of betrayal. While Ruth may not have been betrayed by Naomi in a traditional sense, her story reminds us that our faithfulness to others must be driven by an ultimate faithfulness to God. It will be easy in leadership to misplace loyalty to a person or organization and even easier to surround ourselves by those who will remain loyal to us. But Ruth gently reminds us that seeds sown in allegiance to God will always reap a harvest in the kingdom, no matter who supports or betrays us on earth.

Crucifying scale: Simple steps for sustainability.

Peter said to Jesus, "Rabbi, it is good for us to be here. Let us put up three shelters—one for you, one for Moses and one for Elijah." (He did not know what to say, they were so frightened.) Then a cloud appeared and covered them, and a voice came from the cloud: "This is my Son, whom I love. Listen to him!" Suddenly, when they looked around, they no longer saw anyone with them except Jesus. (Mark 9:5-8)

Peter, James, and John were the disciples closest to Jesus. They were invited into spaces where no one else was allowed: the healing of Jairus's daughter (Mark 5:37), the agony prayer in the Garden of Gethsemane (Matthew 26:37), and, here, the transfiguration of Jesus. They were the ones welcomed in for a closer look at who Jesus was and to witness firsthand the power of what he could do. Being with Jesus was good for them. It enhanced their value and made the shift from being fishermen to becoming fishers of men worthwhile. Over time, they began to realize that they might never enjoy this level of proximity to the miraculous again. So when they experienced the transfiguration of Jesus before their very eyes, they were terrified! The transformation of Jesus from someone like them to someone otherworldly made them realize they were seeing a theophany, a manifestation of the true and living God. According to the Old Testament, they understood that no one could see God and live (Exodus 33:20), so either they were going to die or something big was about to happen. Yet Peter, knowing how good it was to be in the moment, understanding how unique and miraculous Jesus showed himself to be and, according to Mark, not knowing what else to say, suggested that they build altars to forever commemorate what they were experiencing. In a sense, Peter was suggesting that they sustain and scale the transfiguration to make it available and accessible for a longer period of time.

While the desire to make moments and materials more accessible and available for longer is a commendable one, Peter's story reminds us that scale and growth can only happen by the prompting and the hand of God. Peter tried to prompt a project of scale that was initiated by his fear and aided, perhaps, by his desire to make the moment last. But the type of scale God had in mind was far more important than building altars. God did not prompt growth or scale at the transfiguration, but after the ascension of Jesus, the gospel spread to levels that no one could have possibly imagined. When God initiates the scale, it will blow our minds and break through every measurement we could ever dream of. If we truly believe that, then we will be willing to wait for the prompting of the Holy Spirit to show us when to scale for the future and when to remain in the moment.

Scripture is full of examples of people who practiced crucifixion as a means of resurrecting God's glorious intentions. None of them were perfect, but neither are we. Their stories and examples exist to point us to total dependence on the Savior, by the power of God's Spirit at work within us. So, let's breathe in the possibilities of redemptive leadership and breathe out the residue of what we knew before. Let's release the anxieties of trying to measure up and take on the pleasure of knowing that in Christ we are enough. With regular rhythms of letting things go and letting things come, of dying to the world and learning to live for Christ, we might finally find a way to lead with healing and fulfill the wonderful dreams God has envisioned for his world.

EPILOGUE

A Letter to Our Children

I write to you, children, because you know the Father. I write to you, fathers, because you know him who is from the beginning.
I write to you, young people, because you are strong and the word of God abides in you, and you have overcome the evil one.

1 JOHN 2:14 NRSV

I see you.

Designing Roblox games in simulated ease, building Minecraft towers with digital prestige, forming virtual communities where everyone agrees.

I see you fully.

Guiding your friends on where to be and what to play, coordinating matching outfits for spirit day, wearing your confidence that never waivers, no matter what comes your way.

I see you fully leading.

Orchestrating sports teams, winning more than pipe dreams,

Using Pied Piper persuasion to get liars to come clean.

I see you fully leading now.

Develop character today, let integrity guide your way, don't wait till tomorrow to remember you are but clay.

Be weak to find strength, be broken to find healing, let the depth of the cross be your way to break the ceiling.

The world is so dark, the need is too great, please, my daughters and sons, humble yourselves before it's too late.

The beauty of faith is only found in crucifixion, so strengthen your resolve and firm up your convictions.

Believe in the gospel, hold tight to God's truth, never forsake the God of your youth.

For evil abounds and the enemy devours, but you have overcome by God's heavenly powers.

You must fight for the future and lead from the past, be willing to die so your legacy will last.

And when platforms and fame and mountain tops come, remember who you are, never forget where you're from.

You are wise, you are strong, you are an anointed generation. So lead humbly, lead faithfully, lead from every vocation.

The time is now, the laborers are few, and when it gets lonely, remember that God sees you.

I see you.

I see you fully.

I see you fully leading.

I see you fully leading now by the power of God.

ACKNOWLEDGMENTS

God occasionally allows people to corner you so he can catalyze what is within you. This book exists because I was cornered by a discerning and dynamic team at InterVarsity Press: Ed Gilbreath (2018), Al Hsu (2020), Nilwona Nowlin (2023), and president Terumi Echols (2022). Nilwona, my editor and conversation partner, cheered and challenged me from beginning to end. IVP, thank you for trusting me.

I am buoyed by the support of the Soulfire International Ministries board: George Martin, Stephanie McDonald, and my dearest friend, Pastor Eustacia Marshall. My Soulfire sister, Jessica Johnson, has been like a ministry doula: encouraging me to keep pushing to deliver all that God has invested in me through preaching, teaching, writing, and leading with joy.

Annette Hyman, Toni Kim, and Kim Alexander, thank you for counseling me out of my anxieties and guiding me to God's truth. Rev. Enid Almanzar, Hope Dmuchowski, and Cynthia Nwaubani, thank you for reminding me that God's grace makes it possible to be a mom, wife, and executive leader all at the same time.

Bishop Claude Richard Alexander Jr., you are my father in ministry and my partner in crime and calories. Thank you for giving me space to lead and dessert to follow. Tim and Joyce Dalrymple, thank you for validating writing as part of my work and calling at Christianity Today.

Carey Nieuwhof, thank you for partnering with me on this journey. Pete and Geri Scazzero, thank you for infusing within me the DNA of emotionally healthy spirituality.

I am indebted to so many leaders who believed in me, prayed for me, and modeled what it meant to think outside of my traditional boxes. Among those are Pastor Matthew Watley, Dr. William Watley, Bishop Cynthia James, Bishop Walter Scott Thomas, Bishop Kenneth Ulmer, Bishop Vashti McKenzie, Pastor John Jenkins, Christine Caine, Shirley Mullen, Noemi Chavez, Dr. Rodney Cooper, Rabbi Yehiel Poupko, and the late Dr. Joan Parrott. I am better because of you.

Mom and Shelly, thank you for normalizing writing and publishing as "just what we do." Dad would be so proud of us. My extended family is too large to name, but I thank God for the legacies of Estelle Cartledge, Barbara Winstead, Dr. Gwen Cartledge, Mary and Leonard Massie, Albena and Joseph Martin, and all my aunts, uncles, cousins, in-laws, and nieces who flow from their prayers. I honor the generations before me who were kept from education, prevented from learning to read or write, silenced from the pages of history, and forced to forget who God made them to be. I write with you and from you for the glory of God.

To my coach, partner, and closest friend, Dr. Mark Anthony Martin: God overwhelms me daily with his love through you. Thank you for trusting in me when I doubted, for pushing me forward when I wanted to quit, and for reminding me that this work is of the Spirit. Addie and Josie, I can't believe I get to be your mom! As you know, this book is part of your legacy, and I can't wait to see the leaders you will become.

NOTES

INTRODUCTION: THE TIME IS NOW

[1]Michael J. Gorman, "Paul and the Cruciform Way," *Journal of Moral Theology* 2, no. 1 (2013): 64-83.

1. THE REALITIES OF STRESS AND SUFFERING IN OUR PRESENT AGE

[1]Ann Kellett, "The Texas A&M Professor Who Predicted 'the Great Resignation,'" *Texas A&M Today*, February 11, 2022, https://today.tamu.edu/2022/02/11/the-texas-am-professor-who-predicted-the-great-resignation.

[2]Kellett, "The Texas A&M Professor."

[3]Jim Harter, "Is Quiet Quitting Real?," Gallup, May 17, 2023, www.gallup.com/workplace/398306/quiet-quitting-real.aspx.

[4]Harter, "Is Quiet Quitting Real?"

[5]Dana Wilkie, "Today's Young Worker Is Stressed-Out and Anxious," SHRM, September 15, 2020, www.shrm.org/resourcesandtools/hr-topics/employee-relations/pages/young-workers-suffer-from-mental-health-issues.aspx.

[6]MacKenzie R. Peltier et al., "Sex Differences in Stress-Related Alcohol Use," *Neurobiology of Stress* 10 (February 2019), https://doi.org/10.1016/j.ynstr.2019.100149.

[7]Linda Carroll, "More Women in the U.S. Are Drinking Themselves to Death, Research Finds," NBC News, July 28, 2023, www.nbcnews.com/health/womens-health/women-us-are-drinking-death-research-finds-rcna96848.

[8]Kimmy Yam, "Anti-Asian Hate Crimes Increased 339 Percent Nationwide Last Year, Report Says," NBC News, January 31, 2022,

www.nbcnews.com/news/asian-america/anti-asian-hate-crimes
-increased-339-percent-nationwide-last-year-repo-rcna14282.

[9]Ruth Graham, "Antisemitic Incidents Reach New High in U.S., Anti-Defamation League Says," *New York Times,* March 23, 2023, www
.nytimes.com/2023/03/23/us/antisemitism-anti-defamation-league
-report.html.

[10]Michael Dimock and Richard Wike, "America Is Exceptional in the Nature of Its Political Divide," Pew Research Center, November 13, 2020, www
.pewresearch.org/short-reads/2020/11/13/america-is-exceptional
-in-the-nature-of-its-political-divide.

[11]Diane Langberg, *Suffering and the Heart of God: How Trauma Destroys and Christ Restores* (Greensboro, NC: New Growth Press, 2015), 80.

[12]Brené Brown, "Integration Idea: Empathy," Daring Classrooms Hub, accessed July 22, 2024, https://brenebrown.com/wp-content/uploads
/2021/09/Integration-Ideas_Empathy_092221-1.pdf.

[13]Rodney Cooper, "African American Redemptive Leadership," lecture notes, Gordon-Conwell Theological Seminary, 2012.

2. TRIUMPHALISM, TRAUMA, AND THE AMERICAN CHURCH

[1]Alexis de Tocqueville, *Democracy in America: Part II, The Social Influence of Democracy* (New York, 1840), 36-37, available at www.gutenberg.org
/files/816/816-h/816-h.htm.

[2]Paul T. McCartney, "Triumphalism," Encyclopedia.com, accessed July 23, 2024, www.encyclopedia.com/defense/energy-government-and
-defense-magazines/triumphalism.

[3]"Top 10 Richest Countries in the World in 2024 by GPD per Capita," Global Citizen Solutions, updated July 20, 2024, www.globalcitizen
solutions.com/richest-countries-in-the-world.

[4]Brian Blount, *True to Our Native Land: An African American New Testament Commentary* (Minneapolis: Fortress Press, 2007), 523.

[5]Andrew Purves, *The Crucifixion of Ministry: Surrendering Our Ambitions to the Service of Christ* (Downers Grove, IL: InterVarsity Press, 2007), 26.

3. CRUCIFYING POWER

[1]John R. P. French and Bertrand Raven, "The Bases of Social Power," in *Studies in Social Power,* ed. D. Cartwright (Ann Arbor, MI: Institute for

Social Research, 1959), 150-67. Available online at www.communication cache.com/uploads/1/0/8/8/10887248/the_bases_of_social_power _-_chapter_20_-_1959.pdf.

[2] Michigan State University, "DEI Resources: Power & Privilege," MSU Libraries, accessed on July 25, 2024, https://libguides.lib.msu.edu/c .php?g=1133877&p=8276231.

[3] Dartmouth University, Office of Pluralism and Leadership, "Introduction to Power, Privilege, and Social Justice," accessed on July 25, 2023, https://students.dartmouth.edu/opal/education/introduction -power-privilege-and-social-justice.

[4] *Strong's Concordance*, s.v. "power," accessed September 9, 2024, https:// biblehub.net/searchhebrew.php?q=power. Also Annette Griffin, "What Is Dunamis, and What Kind of Power Does Jesus Give Believers?," Bible Study Tools, November 3, 2021, www.biblestudytools.com/bible-study /topical-studies/what-is-dunamis-and-what-kind-of-power-does-jesus -give-believers.html.

4. CRUCIFYING EGO

[1] Mark Leary, "What Is the Ego, and Why Is It So Involved in My Life? The Concept of 'Ego' Is Among the Most Confusing in Psychology," *Psychology Today*, May 13, 2019, www.psychologytoday.com/us/blog/toward -less-egoic-world/201905/what-is-the-ego-and-why-is-it-so-involved -in-my-life.

[2] Robert Shaver, "Egoism," Stanford Encyclopedia of Philosophy, January 9, 2023, https://plato.stanford.edu/entries/egoism.

[3] Ronald E. Riggio, "Are We All Becoming More Self-Centered? What Does This Mean for the Future?" *Psychology Today*, July 27, 2017, www .psychologytoday.com/us/blog/cutting-edge-leadership/201707/are -we-all-becoming-more-self-centered?

[4] Alison Gray, "Worldviews," *International Psychiatry* 8, no. 3 (2011): 58-60, www.ncbi.nlm.nih.gov/pmc/articles/PMC6735033.

[5] For a practical assessment of your worldview, see www.knowledgeworkx .com/framework-three-colors-of-worldview.

[6] "Personality," American Psychological Association, accessed on July 25, 2024, www.apa.org/topics/personality.

[7] David Marcum and Steven Smith, *Egonomics: What Makes Ego Our Greatest Asset (or Most Expensive Liability)* (New York: Fireside, 2008).

[8]Dana Wilkie, "Let It Go: Teaching a Micromanager How to Chill," SHRM, March 31, 2020, www.shrm.org/topics-tools/news/employee -relations/let-go-teaching-micromanager-how-to-chill.

5. CRUCIFYING SPEED

[1]James C. Cobb, "What We Can Learn from Coca-Cola's Biggest Blunder," *Time*, July 10, 2015, https://time.com/3950205/new-coke -history-america.

[2]Mark Pendergrast, *For God, Country and Coca-Cola: The Definitive History of the Great American Soft Drink and the Company That Makes It,* rev. and exp. ed. (New York: Basic Books, 2004), 355.

[3]"New Coke: The Most Memorable Marketing Blunder Ever?" accessed on July 25, 2024, www.coca-colacompany.com/about-us/history/new -coke-the-most-memorable-marketing-blunder-ever.

[4]Cobb, "What We Can Learn."

[5]"How Coca-Cola is Rethinking Disruptive Innovation to Anticipate To-morrow's Tastes," *Yumda*, February 20, 2022, www.yumda.com/en/news /1165064/how-coca-cola-is-rethinking-disruptive-innovation-to-anticipate -tomorrows-tastes.html.

6. CRUCIFYING PERFORMANCE

[1]Ben Wigert and Annamarie Mann, "Give Performance Reviews That Actually Inspire Employees," Gallup Workplace, September 25, 2017, www.gallup.com/workplace/236135/give-performance-reviews -actually-inspire-employees.aspx.

[2]All names, characters, and incidents portrayed in this story are ficti-tious. No identification with actual persons (living or deceased), places, buildings, and products is intended or should be inferred.

[3]Kristi Hedges, *The Power of Presence: Unlocking Your Potential to Influence and Engage Others* (New York: AMACOM, 2012), 10.

[4]Luis Costa, "Become a Fully Present Leader and Human Through the Four Selves," Forbes, February 1, 2022, www.forbes.com/sites/forbes coachescouncil/2022/02/01/become-a-fully-present-leader-and -human-through-the-four-selves/.

7. CRUCIFYING PERFECTION

[1] Gail Cornwall, "Perfectionism Can Become a Vicious Cycle in Families," *The Atlantic*, July 19, 2021, www.theatlantic.com/family/archive /2021/07/family-other-oriented-perfectionism-parents-child/619461.

[2] Mary M. Christopher and Jennifer Shewmaker, "The Relationship of Perfectionism to Affective Variables in Gifted and Highly Able Children," *Gifted Child Today* 33, no. 3 (Summer 2010), https://files.eric .ed.gov/fulltext/EJ893803.pdf.

[3] Kelly Hillock and Stephanie Zumwalt, "5 Things You Didn't Know About Mozart," San Diego Symphony, accessed on July 25, 2024, www .sandiegosymphony.org/blog/5-things-you-didnt-know-zart -about-mozart.

[4] Rob Haskell, "Serena Williams Says Farewell to Tennis on Her Own Terms—and in Her Own Words," *Vogue*, August 9, 2022, www.vogue .com/article/serena-williams-retirement-in-her-own-words.

[5] Thomas Curran and Andrew P. Hill, "Perfectionism Is Increasing, and That's Not Good News," *Harvard Business Review*, January 26, 2018, https://hbr.org/2018/01/perfectionism-is-increasing-and-thats -not-good-news.

[6] Rebecca Greenfield, "The Crazy Perfectionism That Drove Steve Jobs," *The Atlantic*, November 7, 2011, www.theatlantic.com/technology /archive/2011/11/crazy-perfectionism-drove-steve-jobs/335842.

[7] Greenfield, "The Crazy Perfectionism."

[8] Rebecca Knight, "How to Manage Your Perfectionism," *Harvard Business Review*, April 29, 2019, https://hbr.org/2019/04/how-to-manage-your -perfectionism.

8. CRUCIFYING LOYALTY

[1] All names, characters, and incidents portrayed in this story are fictitious. No identification with actual persons (living or deceased), places, buildings, and products is intended or should be inferred.

[2] Kate Shellnutt, "Former Mars Hill Elders: Mark Driscoll Is Still 'Unrepentant,' Unfit to Pastor," *Christianity Today*, July 26, 2021, www .christianitytoday.com/news/2021/july/mars-hill-elders-letter-mark -driscoll-pastor-resign-trinity.html.

[3] Max De Pree, *Leadership Is an Art* (East Lansing: Michigan State University Press, 1987).

9. CRUCIFYING SCALE

[1]Chad Glasscock, "Growth vs. Scaling—What's the Difference?," LinkedIn, February 4, 2021, www.linkedin.com/pulse/growth-vs-scaling -whats-difference-chad-glasscock.

[2]"The Moving Assembly Line and the Five-Dollar Workday," Ford, accessed on July 25, 2024, https://corporate.ford.com/articles/history /moving-assembly-line.html.

[3]"The Union Stockyards: A Story of American Capitalism," WTTW, accessed July 25, 2024, https://interactive.wttw.com/chicago-stories /union-stockyards/the-union-stockyards-a-story-of-american-capitalism.

[4]"The Union Stockyards."

[5]Patrick Vlaskovits, "Henry Ford, Innovation, and That 'Faster Horse' Quote," *Harvard Business Review,* August 29, 2011, https://hbr.org /2011/08/henry-ford-never-said-the-fast.

[6]Gayle Faulkner Kosalko, "The History of White Castle," Whiting-Robertsdale Historical Society, accessed July 25, 2024, www.wrhistorical society.com/white-castle.

[7]Kansas Historical Society, "Walter Anderson," January 2016, www.kshs .org/kansapedia/walter-anderson/17828.

[8]Callum Glennen, "The Rise of McDonald's: From Super Sized Criticism to Progressive Burger Company," World Finance, accessed July 25, 2024, www.worldfinance.com/markets/the-rise-of-mcdonalds-from-super -sized-criticism-to-progressive-burger-company.

[9]Marilyn Haigh, "Why White Castle Isn't a Fast-Food Giant," CNBC, November 19, 2019, www.cnbc.com/2019/11/19/why-white-castle-is-losing -to-mcdonalds-and-burger-king.html.

[10]Scott Neuman, "Megachurches Are Getting Even Bigger as Churches Close Across the Country," NPR, July 14, 2023, www.npr.org/2023 /07/14/1187460517/megachurches-growing-liquid-church.

[11]David Garrison, *Church Planting Movements: How God Is Redeeming a Lost World* (Monument, CO: WIGTake Resources, 2004).

[12]*Wall Street,* directed by Oliver Stone (Los Angeles: 20th Century Fox, 1987).

[13]Adam Hayes, "Bernie Madoff: Who He Was and How His Ponzi Scheme Worked," Investopedia, June 23, 2024, www.investopedia.com/terms /b/bernard-madoff.asp.

10. RESURRECTING HEALING AND HOPE

[1]John Maxwell, *The 21 Irrefutable Laws of Leadership: Follow Them and People Will Follow You* (New York: HarperCollins Leadership, 2022).

[2]I first heard this phrase from a sermon preached by Rev. Dr. Eustacia Marshall in 2016 in reference to Genesis 37.

[3]Elizaveta Solomonova, "Dreams Are Made of Pasts and Futures," *Psychology Today*, June 11, 2022, www.psychologytoday.com/us/blog/mind-states/202206/dreams-are-made-pasts-and-futures.

Like this book?
Scan the code to discover more content like this!

Get on IVP's email list to receive special offers, exclusive book news, and thoughtful content from your favorite authors on topics you care about.

 | InterVarsity Press

IVPRESS.COM/BOOK-QR